Heroes in History

*A Practical K–12 Curriculum
for Creating a More Inclusive, Equitable,
and Culturally Proficient Campus*

Stephanie Bazzell

Heroes in History: A Practical K–12 Curriculum for Creating a More Inclusive, Equitable, and Culturally Proficient Campus © 2020 Stephanie Bazzell

Paperback ISBN: 978-1-948361-30-9

Cover Art & Design by Fantasy & Coffee Design: Fantasy & Coffee Design

Editing: Lyss Em

Formatting: Phycel Designs

All rights reserved. No parts of this publication may be reproduced, stored in a retrieval system, or transmitted in any form or by any means, electronic, mechanical, photocopying, recording, or otherwise, without the prior written permission of the copyright owner. Teachers may make copies for their students.

Contents

Introduction	vi
Charles Henry Turner	2
Bessie Coleman	4
Jovita Idár	6
Vera Rubin	8
Mae Jemison	10
Patsy Takemoto Mink	12
Peter Salem	14
Octavia Spencer	16
Annie Malone Turnbo	18
Lizzie Velásquez	20
Marie Tharp	22
Urvashi Vaid	24
Gwendolyn Brooks	26
Ada Lovelace	28
Zitkála-Šá	30
Luisa Moreno	32
Joseph Henry Douglass	34
Temple Grandin	36
Nanyehi	38
Frances Perkins	40
Shirley Ann Jackson	42
Jo Ann Robinson	44
Marie Maynard Daly	46
Raffi Freedman-Gurspan	48
Nella Larsen	50
Sarah Winnemucca	52
Mary Fields	54
Mona Hanna-Attisha	56
Felicitas Gómez Martínez de Mendez	58
Tammy Duckworth	60
Granville Woods	62
Linda Sarsour	64
Elouise Cobell	66
Ralph Lazo	68
Lou Sullivan	70
Farida Bedwei	72
Amanda Nguyen	74
About the Author	77
Bibliography	79

Acknowledgments

This project was inspired during the summer of 2020. I knew I wanted to make a difference. Throughout the 2020–2021 school year, I would often have doubts if this would really help, but talking with the students always gave me encouragement. I knew it was only a drop in the bucket of change, but if everyone keeps dripping, the bucket will one day overflow. I especially want to thank Amy Obenhaus, who allowed this project to get off the ground. Also, a big thank-you to Sholonda Miller. She was an ever-encouraging source of joy throughout the year. Also, Sabine Watts, Greg Marquardt, and my editor, Lyss Em.

Introduction

Our classrooms are more diverse than ever, but so many teachers struggle to develop lessons that connect with their students. The *Heroes in History* curriculum is built around students and gives them weekly heroes who reflect the diverse classroom of today. These historical and contemporary figures were chosen specifically to span a wide range of people. Each one initiates a different subject that will allow discussion on issues impacting our students today. There is one hero per week, for a total of thirty-eight weeks.

The teacher facilitates the conversation, allowing a safe space for students to learn about these heroes and giving students the language to talk about these important issues.

What to Do

A school-wide announcement should be made about the hero of the week. Tuesday is the best day, since holidays often fall on Mondays. The announcement helps create a campus culture of the importance of recognizing these heroes.

The teacher will read the biography page of the hero of the week with students. The short biography is meant to inspire further research into the hero. Discussion questions can be answered throughout the week, with teacher-created extension activities added if needed. Discussion questions are purposely designed to first enable the students to connect with the hero before learning into more culturally focused questions. Some questions will require research and might not be answered in one day. Discussion fosters community and will help teachers build rapport with students. Depending on student ages and abilities, more scaffolding with discussions will be necessary. All questions, even difficult ones, should be discussed. Students will understand the question at their level and have a right to be challenged to think deeply. Scaffolding methods can be increased or decreased depending on students' level. Kindergarten might spend several days reading and discussing the biography, while high school may be able to read and complete discussion in a single day. Extra reading for both students and teachers can be found in the back of the book in the works cited section.

Teachers may select a picture of the hero from the internet or have students illustrate a hero poster. The picture should be placed in the classroom and kept up for the school year. Each week, the new hero picture is added. It is good to come back to and remind students about past heroes.

Appropriate hallways should have displays of each hero of the week with "At (School name) we remember…" with the pictures following.

Common Questions

Do I really have to talk about racism and sexism with elementary students?

YES. Racism and sexism affect students even before they are born. If they are old enough to have these things affect them, they are old enough to learn about them. As students get older, they will develop a deeper understanding of the world, but it is necessary for the first exposure to the words to be in a safe and supportive classroom.

How do I explain racism and sexism to students? They are always asking me why people are like that.

Describe it how Charles Henry Turner did. It is an unconditioned response to someone unfamiliar and through learned behavior by imitating others.

Charles Henry Turner

Announcement

Do you know about Charles Henry Turner? He was born February 3, 1867, two years after the Civil War. In 1907 he earned his doctorate in zoology from the University of Chicago, becoming the first African American to earn a doctorate from the school. Due the racist practice of segregation, he had a difficult time finding a position at a major university. Eventually he found a science teaching position at a segregated high school. Lacking the use of the laboratory, he conducted his research at nearby parks. He was the first person to prove insects can hear. He discovered cockroaches can learn and that honeybees can see colors and patterns.

At (SCHOOL NAME) we remember Charles Henry Turner, and now you, too, can explore animals in their surroundings and discover something new.

Discussion Questions

- Charles's parents encouraged him to read. Is there anything your parents encourage you to do?

- What animals and insects are in your local area? Have you seen any animals around your school?

- How many years after Charles Henry Turner was born did segregation finally come to an end? Why do you think it took so long?

- A picture book about Charles called Buzzing with Questions: The Inquisitive Mind of Charles Henry Turner is out. What do you think the book is about? Why might Charles be a good topic for a book?

- If Charles had been given the same resources as his white peers in university, how might his discoveries have been different? How might his life have changed?

- What do you think of Charles's theory about racism? What do you do to combat racism?

Charles Henry Turner

Charles Henry Turner was born February 3, 1867, two years after the Civil War. His father was a church custodian, and his mother was a nurse. They encouraged Charles to read and learn. He was valedictorian of his high school class and enrolled in the University of Cincinnati. There he earned a master's in biology. He was the first African American to earn a graduate degree from the school.

Charles married Leontine Troy in 1886. Charles admired the work of evolutionary biologists Charles Darwin and George Romanes so much he named one of his children Darwin Romanes after them. Leontine died in 1895, and Charles remarried a few years later to Lillian Porter Turner.

Charles began his doctorate at Denison University. Due to racism, he had a difficult time finding a position at a major university. Eventually, he was able to get a position at the historically Black college, Clark College. In 1907 he earned his doctorate in zoology from the University of Chicago. He graduated magna cum laude and was the first African American to earn a doctorate there. Eventually, he found a science teaching position in St. Louis, Missouri, at Sumner High School, a segregated school.

While teaching, he pioneered research techniques for animal behavior science. He made many notable discoveries despite lacking the basic use of laboratory space and research assistants that his white peers had in their university positions. Most of his experiments were conducted at nearby parks.

Charles contributed over seventy papers on a wide range of topics. He was the first person to prove insects can hear. He discovered cockroaches can learn and that honeybees can see colors and patterns. He believed in the importance of observing insects in the wild, concluding that studying them in the lab can create artificial results.

Charles held a commitment to civil rights and was an activist in St. Louis. He believed only through education could people change their racist behavior. He theorized racism existed because of an unconditioned response to someone unfamiliar and through learned behavior by imitating others.

He died in Chicago in 1923. The Turner Middle School in St. Louis was named in his honor, and Charles's story continues inspiring others to explore animals in their surroundings.

Bessie Coleman

Announcement

Do you know about Bessie Coleman? She was born in 1892 and was part African American and part Native American. At a young age, her family moved to Waxahachie, Texas. She loved math and wanted to become a pilot, but American flight schools refused to allow women or Blacks to attend. So she learned French, moved to Paris, and in 1921 became the first Black woman and first Native American to earn a pilot's license. She returned to the US, where she became a media sensation performing stunt tricks at flying shows.

At (SCHOOL NAME) we remember Bessie Coleman and hope you, too, will soar to your dreams.

Discussion Questions

- What is sharecropping? Do you think it's an unfair practice? Why or why not? How might it be improved?
- How far is your school from your home?
- What is stunt flying? Do you think you would be brave enough to do it?
- Why do you think that in France Bessie could get her pilot's license but she couldn't in the US?
- What impact do you think Bessie had in the US?

Bessie Coleman

Bessie Coleman was born on January 26, 1892. She was part Cherokee and part African American. When she was young, her family moved to Waxahachie, Texas, and lived as sharecroppers.

She would walk four miles, both ways, to go to her segregated, one-room schoolhouse. She was a brilliant student and loved math and reading.

At the age of twenty-three, Bessie moved to Chicago, Illinois. After hearing stories about flying from returning World War I soldiers, she dreamed of becoming a pilot. She worked as a manicurist and at a chili parlor to save money for her dream. She was unable to earn her pilot's license in the United States because of systemic racism and sexism. American flight schools did not admit Blacks or women.

Other parts of the world were more accepting. Bessie took a French-language class and in 1920 moved to Paris. There she became the first Black woman and first Native American to earn an aviation pilot's license. She specialized in stunt flying and parachuting.

Back in the US, she captivated audiences. After all, she became the first African American woman in America to make a public flight. To earn extra money to buy her own plane, Bessie opened a beauty shop in Orlando, Florida.

Bessie used her popularity to promote aviation and combat racism. She refused to take part in any flying shows that prohibited African Americans from attending. She was offered a movie deal, but when she arrived on set to learn that the movie's first scene had her appear in tattered clothes, with a pack on her back and a walking stick, she left the set. She refused to perpetuate the racist stereotype most whites had of Blacks.

She wanted to establish a flying school for Blacks; unfortunately, she did not live long enough to achieve this goal. A wrench got stuck in the engine of the plane Bessie was a passenger on, and it crashed. She died on April 30, 1926.

Today Bessie Coleman is recognized for her accomplishments in aviation. She was number 14 on *Flying*'s 2013 list "51 Heroes of Aviation." There are several Bessie Coleman scholarships for high school seniors planning for careers in aviation.

Jovita Idár

Announcement

Do you know about Jovita Idár? She was a Mexican American nurse, teacher, journalist, and civil rights activist. She was born Laredo, Texas, in 1885. During her first year of teaching, she became frustrated by the lack of supplies at her segregated schools. So she became an editor and writer for *La Crónica*, a Mexican American newspaper focusing on news and civil rights. Exercising her first amendment rights, she published an editorial criticizing President Woodrow Wilson. The Texas Rangers did not like her speaking out and wrongfully went to close the newspaper's office. When they arrived Jovita Idár stood in the front door and refused to let them in.

At (SCHOOL NAME) we remember Jovita Idár and hope you, too, will do what you can to help others.

Discussion Questions

- How do you think being one of eight children impacted Jovita? Would her life have looked different if her family had not been wealthy?

- Do you agree with Jovita's idea that she would have more impact on her students as a journalist than as a teacher? Why or why not?

- Why do you think the Texas Rangers shut down the newspaper? What could they have done differently to keep with the law?

- How did the Texas Rangers treat Mexican and Mexican American people during Jovita's lifetime?

Jovita Idár

Jovita Idár was a Mexican American woman born on September 7, 1885, in Laredo, Texas. She was one of eight children and came from a privileged family. Because of this, she was able to get many opportunities that other Mexican Americans were not able to. Growing up, Jovita won prizes for her poetry.

Jovita earned her teaching certificate in 1903. She worked at a segregated school for Mexican American students. Her students did not have enough textbooks, pens, or paper for their lessons. Jovita realized her teaching made little impact on her students' lives. So she decided to become a journalist and activist.

She worked with her two brothers for their father's newspaper, *La Crónica*. Jovita wrote articles exposing the poor living conditions of other Mexican Americans. At the time, Mexican Americans faced much social discrimination and lynching. She also wrote about the poor education conditions Mexican Americans received even though they paid the same taxes as whites.

While writing news stories for *La Crónica*, Jovita would write under different pseudonyms. She and her brother fought for Mexican civil rights and for women's suffrage. *La Crónica* also established the First Mexican Congress, an organization dedicated to fighting inequalities and racism as well as uniting Mexicans on issues of economic resources and fighting against their lack of access to adequate education.

Jovita used her first amendment rights and wrote an editorial criticizing President Woodrow Wilson. It offended the Texas Rangers, and they illegally attempted to close the newspaper. She stood in the entryway and refused to let them in. They later returned and shut down the paper when she was not there.

Jovita also served as the first president for the League of Mexican Women. The organization offered free education to Mexican children. In addition, Jovita pioneered the idea that children's classes should be taught in both English and Spanish.

In 1921 she moved to San Antonio and continued to promote equal rights for women. She volunteered in a hospital, interpreting for Spanish-speaking patients, and even founded a free kindergarten. She never had children, but she did help raise the children of her sister who died in childbirth.

Jovita died on June 15, 1946.

Vera Rubin

Announcement

Do you know about Vera Rubin? She was born in 1928 to two Jewish immigrants. At a young age, she enjoyed science and observing the stars. She became an astronomer and provided the first direct evidence of the existence of dark matter. Twenty-seven percent of the universe is made from dark matter. It affects how stars move within galaxies and how objects clump together. Vera's research of dark matter is one of the most important discoveries within physics.

At (SCHOOL NAME) we remember Vera Rubin and know that you, too, can aim for the stars.

Discussion Questions

- Are you able to see the stars from your home? How is light pollution impacting the night sky?
- What kinds of books do you like to check out from the library?
- What were some of the unnecessary struggles Vera had to face because she was a woman? Do you think these still happen today? Why or why not?
- How could the universities and observatories have been more welcoming to women?

Vera Rubin

Vera Rubin was born July 23, 1928, to two Jewish immigrants. When Vera was ten years old, she became interested in astronomy. She watched the stars using a cardboard telescope she built with her father. She checked out science books from the library and would even write English papers on topics related to the stars.

Vera earned her bachelor's degree in astronomy in 1948. She wanted to further her education by attended the graduate program at Princeton, but because of sexism, Princeton would not allow women astronomy students. So she attended the universities Cornell and Georgetown, since they would. Throughout her studies, she faced many unnecessary struggles due to sexism. One time, she could not meet her adviser in his office because women were not allowed in that part of the building.

Vera married and had four children. Vera's husband would wait in the car while she attended night classes at Cornell.

In 1965 Vera studied the rotation of galaxies at the Palomar Observatory and became the first women to observe there. The only restroom at the observatory was labeled for men. So she drew a skirted person and pasted it over the door.

She battled to gain credibility as a woman. Many of her early papers were dismissed by her male colleagues even though her research ultimately proved to be valid.

Determined, she continued her research and provided the first direct evidence of the existence of dark matter. Twenty-seven percent of the universe is made from dark matter. It affects how stars move within galaxies and how objects clump together. Vera's research of dark matter is one of the most important discoveries within physics.

Vera always encouraged girls to investigate the universe and study science. She believed that cultural factors were to blame for preventing some women from going into science. She would call conference organizers and point out when women speakers were being underrepresented.

She died on December 25, 2016. In 2019 an observatory in Chile was named after her. The observatory focuses on the study of dark matter and dark energy.

Mae Jemison

Announcement

Do you know about Mae Jemison? On September 28, 1989, she became the first Black woman in space. Growing up, Mae enjoyed studying human biology and dancing. At sixteen she graduated high school and attended Stanford University, where she earned a degree in chemical engineering and a degree in African and African American studies. She became a doctor and on her space flight, studied bone cells. Back on Earth she opened many businesses, including a space camp for kids. Mae currently lives in Houston, Texas.

Here at (SCHOOL NAME) we remember Mae Jemison.

Discussion Questions

- Are there any shows you watch with characters you look up to? Explain.
- What are some of your passions? Can you do all these when you grow up?
- What's something in the human body that you are curious about?
- What other languages do you wish you could speak?
- If you were going into space, what photos would you take with you?

Mae Jemison

Mae Jemison was born on October 17, 1956. When she was a child, she enjoyed nature and human biology. She would watch the TV show *Star Trek*. Seeing a Black actress play a lieutenant on the show further sparked Mae's interest in space. When the first space flight happened, Mae was irritated that there were no women astronauts.

Mae also loved to dance and learned several styles of dance from African and Japanese to ballet and jazz. Growing up, she wanted to become a professional dancer.

She studied hard and did well in school. She graduated high school when she was only sixteen and attended Stanford University. She served as head of the Black Student Union and choreographed musicals and dances. During her senior year, she struggled with choosing between going to medical school and being a professional dancer. In 1977 she earned her bachelor's degree in chemical engineering and a degree in African and African American studies.

Mae attended medical school at Cornell. After getting her medical degree, she joined the Peace Corps. Later, she also worked for the Centers for Disease Control, helping with research for various vaccines.

In 1987 she joined NASA, and on September 12, 1992, she became the first Black woman in space. She carried a photo of Bessie Coleman and a poster from the Alvin Ailey American Dance Theater. In space Mae studied bone cells and how tadpoles develop in zero gravity.

In 1993 Mae retired from NASA and used her platform of former astronaut to speak out on getting more minorities interested in science. She opened businesses, including a science camp for children. She became a professor at many colleges and wrote many books, including *Finding Where the Wind Goes* and a book series about space called True Book. In 1993 she even acted in an episode of *Star Trek: The Next Generation*.

Along with English, Mae is fluent in Russian, Japanese, and Swahili. She never gave up her love of dance and created a dance studio in her home. Mae currently lives in Houston, Texas.

Patsy Takemoto Mink

Announcement

Do you know about Patsy Takemoto Mink? She was a third-generation Japanese American and as a child enjoyed playing football and baseball with her brother. In 1946 Patsy attended the University of Nebraska and formed a coalition of students. Together they pressured the university to stop its racist practice of dorm segregation. She became a lawyer and in 1965 became the first woman of color elected to the US House of Representatives.

At (SCHOOL NAME) we remember Patsy Takemoto Mink.

Discussion Questions

- What kinds of things do people encourage you to do?
- How might Patsy's life have been different if she hadn't been born into privilege?
- Why is segregation inherently unequal? How many years before public segregation was banned in the US did Patsy and her classmates desegregate the dorms?
- How did sexism impact Patsy's life?
- Of the bills Patsy helped pass, what one do you think has the biggest impact in your life?

Patsy Takemoto Mink

Patsy Takemoto Mink was born on December 6, 1927, in Hawaii. She was a third-generation Japanese American and was born into privilege compared to other Japanese American people in the area. Her parents encouraged her to be strong and assertive. She would play football and baseball with her brother. In high school Patsy served as president of the student body, making her the first girl president at her high school.

In 1946 Patsy attended the University of Nebraska. The school had a racist policy forcing her, along with all other nonwhite students, to live in segregated dorms. Patsy organized and created a coalition of students who pushed for equal rights. The coalition successfully lobbied the university to end their segregation policy.

She earned a bachelor's degree in zoology and chemistry in 1948. She then applied for medical school, but because she was a woman, all her applications were rejected. So she went to law school at the University of Chicago, where she earned her law degree. There was only one other woman in her class.

Patsy had trouble finding work as a lawyer. She was an Asian American woman in an interracial marriage and had a child. All the practices she applied for were simply too racist or sexist to hire her. With the help of her father, she established a private firm and began to teach law classes at the University of Hawaii.

In 1965 Patsy won a seat in the US House of Representatives, becoming the first woman of color elected to the House. She helped drive issues on children, education, and gender equality. Some programs she helped establish include Head Start, school lunch, and bilingual education.

Patsy died of pneumonia on September 28, 2002, at age seventy-four. Her death occurred one week after she won the primary election. It was too late to remove her name from the general election ballot. On November 5, 2020, Patsy won the reelection. Her seat was filled by Ed Case after a special election. Her hard work and determination continue to inspire people today.

Peter Salem

Announcement

Peter Salem was born into slavery on October 1, 1750. Peter was granted his freedom when he enlisted in the Massachusetts Minutemen. He was one of over five thousand African American soldiers who fought for American independence during the Revolutionary War. He fought in the Battles of Lexington and Concord, Bunker Hill, Saratoga, and Stony Point. During the Battle of Bunker Hill, Peter mortally wounded the British Major.

At (SCHOOL NAME) we remember Peter Salem.

Discussion Questions

- What events led up to the American Revolution? How did the fear of slave abolishment impact the wealthy white male leaders of the US?
- Who is Crispus Attucks? What impact did his death have on Black Americans during the Revolutionary War?
- Why do you think Black soldiers fought longer in the war?
- How did slavery change after the American Revolution?

Peter Salem

Peter Salem was born into slavery on October 1, 1750. In 1775 his master freed him so Peter could fight in the Massachusetts Minutemen during the American Revolution.

Many people were divided between wanting America to stay a part of England and wanting to form their own country. Many Blacks fought, for both sides of the revolution. Most believed victory by the British would lead to an end to slavery. The British promised freedom to enslaved Blacks, and over twenty thousand enslaved people escaped and fought for the British Army.

Over nine thousand Black soldiers fought for America during the revolution. Five thousand of them were combat dedicated troops, while the others worked as guides, messengers, and spies.

The war took over eight years, and between 200,000 and 250,000 men served for America. Black Soldiers made up about 4 percent, but they fought eight times longer than the average white soldier.

Peter fought in many battles, including the Battles of Lexington and Concord, Bunker Hill, Saratoga, and Stony Point. At the Battle of Bunker Hill, Peter mortally wounded British Marine Major John Pitcairn.

After the war, in 1783, Peter married Katy Benson in Salem, Massachusetts. He built a cabin near Leicester and worked as a cane weaver. He died on August 16, 1816, at the age of sixty-six. He was buried in Framingham, and the town erected a monument in his memory in 1882.

Octavia Spencer

Announcement

Do you know about Octavia Spencer? She played the NASA mathematician Dorothy Vaughan in the movie *Hidden Figures*. Octavia is also the author of the book series Randi Rhodes, Ninja Detective. It might surprise you to learn that Octavia is dyslexic. As a child she would become paralyzed with fear when called to read aloud in class. Octavia was a gifted auditory learner, and her teachers helped her work toward her strengths. She believes there are no limitations in life except for the ones people place on themselves.

At (SCHOOL NAME) we remember Octavia Spencer and will help you develop your strengths.

Discussion Questions

- What do you think the statement "there are no limitations on people's lives expect for the limitations they place on themselves" means? Do you agree or disagree? Why?
- Do you like reading aloud in class?
- What are some of your strengths? How can you use them when you study for class?
- What are some strategies used to help people with dyslexia?
- Why do you think Octavia reading her books for an audio recording was bittersweet?

Octavia Spencer

Octavia Spencer was born on May 25, 1970. She was one of seven children. Her father died when she was thirteen. Octavia's mom was strict but supportive. Her mother would often say there were no limitations on people's lives expect for the limitations they placed on themselves.

In school Octavia learned she had dyslexia. She would become paralyzed with fear when she was called on to read aloud in class. She would invert letters and drop words while she read. She knew she was a smart kid and hated feeling that she was not as smart as the others. Octavia was a gifted auditory learner and could solve problems faster than the other students. Her teachers helped her learn to adapt to her dyslexia and work toward her strengths.

She earned a degree in English with a double minor in journalism and theater from Auburn University. In high school she wanted to work behind the camera in movies. So she moved to Los Angeles after she graduated. The first movie she worked on was called *A Time to Kill*. She had been hired to work with casting but asked if she could audition for a part. She was successful and landed the part of a nurse.

Currently Octavia has acted in over one hundred movies and TV shows. She's written and directed two short films and holds over ten producing credits. She is one of two women of color to have received three Oscar nominations.

In 2013 Octavia became an author. She wrote two books in the Randi Rhodes, Ninja Detective series: *The Case of the Time-Capsule Bandit* and *The Sweetest Heist in History*. When she recorded the audio versions of the books, the fear of reading aloud came back. She described the process as bittersweet with more sweet than bitter. Dyslexia doesn't go away with age.

Octavia worked toward her strengths and learned ways to strive with dyslexia. She still acts and produces movies today.

Annie Malone Turnbo

Announcement

Do you know about Annie Malone Turnbo? She was an African American businesswoman and inventor. In school she enjoyed chemistry and later combined it with her passion for hair care. She invented several hair straightening treatments that wouldn't damage a person's hair or scalp. People loved her products. By the 1920s she'd become a multimillionaire and is thought to be the first African American woman millionaire in the US. Annie believed the wealthy should give away most of their fortunes, and she gave to many local organizations to help her community.

Here at (SCHOOL NAME) we remember Annie Malone Turnbo.

Discussion Questions

- List a few things you are learning in school that interest you.
- What are some hair products you or people in your family use?
- How could Annie have protected herself and her company from her ex-husband?
- What do you think of Annie's belief that the wealthy should give away most of their fortunes?
- What is a living wage?
- What does it mean to live modestly?

Annie Turnbo Malone

Annie Turnbo Malone was born on August 9, 1877. She was the daughter of Robert and Isabella Turnbo, who were both formerly enslaved people. Her father fought for the Union in the Civil War.

Annie became an orphan at a young age and lived with her older sister. In high school Annie enjoyed learning chemistry and practicing hairdressing with her sister. She took her interest in chemistry and combined it with her passion for hair and hair care. In time, Annie developed a chemical process for nondamaging hair straighteners and oils for Black hair. At the time, many people would use heavy oils and soaps to straighten their curls, but they would hurt their scalps and hair. Annie's formula strengthened hair and prevented damage.

In 1902 she moved to St. Louis and hired three assistants to sell her hair-care products door-to-door. One of the assistances was Madam C. J. Walker, who became another pioneering Black businesswoman in hair care. Annie would give away free treatments to attract more customers. Her business was in such high demand she opened a shop on Main Street.

In 1918 Annie established Poro College, a cosmetology school and center. The school curriculum addressed the whole student, from dress to maintaining integrity, along with cosmetology.

Annie became a multimillionaire, making her one of the first Black women millionaires in the US. She lived modestly and believed that wealthy people should give away most of their money. She gave thousands of dollars to the local Black YMCA and the Howard University College of Medicine. She also gave to a local orphans' home. The home was later renamed in her honor. Annie also believed in giving her workers living wages and opportunities for advancement.

In 1927 her then husband filed for divorce. He was president of Annie's company and, despite not being there from the beginning, demanded half of her business. She fought him in court, won, and maintained full ownership of her business. The Great Depression hit, and most businesses in the US folded. Though reduced in size, Annie's still thrived.

On May 10, 1957, Annie died of a stroke. Netflix created a fictionalized version of Annie's and Madam C. J. Walker's lives in the show *Self Made*. Octavia Spencer acted as the lead.

Lizzie Velásquez

Announcement

Do you know about Lizzie Velásquez? She was born on March 13, 1989, in Austin, Texas. She has a rare genetic condition that makes her unable to gain weight. When Lizzie was seventeen, she found a YouTube video that called her "the world's ugliest woman." She was mad and upset but knew she couldn't allow other people to define her. Today Lizzie is a college graduate, an author of over four books, a motivational speaker, and an anti-bullying activist.

At (SCHOOL NAME) we remember Lizzie Velásquez and know you, too, can prevent bullying.

Discussion Questions

- What is one thing that makes you different from the other kids in your classroom?
- Why do you think Lizzie's parents did not want her to feel different? Do you think engaging people who would stare was a good or bad idea? How might it have helped or hurt?
- Do you think the people who wrote the cruel comments in the YouTube video about Lizzie would say the same things to her in person? How might they have acted differently if they had known Lizzie?
- What do you think about the way Lizzie's friends confronted people who would talk bad about her? What can you do when you see/hear people being bullied in your school?
- What are some things you want to accomplish in life?
- What does the idea that "you get to decide how you want to define yourself to the world" mean to you?
- How can Lizzie's story motivate others?

Lizzie Velásquez

Lizzie Velásquez was born on March 13, 1989, in Austin, Texas. She has a very rare condition called Marfan lipodystrophy syndrome. Only one other person is believed to also have this genetic condition. Lizzie is unable to gain weight and has never weighed more than sixty-three pounds even as an adult. She is also blind in one eye, but she has never let her condition get in the way of her dreams.

While Lizzie was growing up, her parents would not let her feel different. If an adult or child would stare at Lizzie, her parents would ask if the person wanted to say hi and strike up a conversation. It wasn't until Lizzie started school and the other kids looked at her like she was a monster did she realize she was different. When she got home, she cried, but her mom told her the only difference between her and the other kids was that she was small. Lizzie went to school the next day smiling and showing the other kids she was just like them.

It wasn't always easy—some days Lizzie wished she could scrub off her syndrome and look like everyone else—but she wasn't going to let her condition define her. She joined cheerleading, yearbook, and even the drama club while in high school. She had many awesome friends who supported her. If they heard someone commenting on Lizzie's appearance, they would go up to the person and say how Lizzie was their friend and fun to be around.

When Lizzie was seventeen, she found a YouTube video that called her "the world's ugliest woman." The comments on the video were also exceedingly cruel, one even saying she should kill herself. These people knew nothing about Lizzie, only that she looked different. She was mad and upset but knew she couldn't allow other people to define her. She would use those negative comments to fuel her drive. On that day, she decided she wanted to be a motivational speaker, write a book, and graduate from college.

She graduated college with an English degree and in 2010 published a book with her mother in English and Spanish called *Lizzie Beautiful: The Lizzie Velásquez Story*. She wrote two other books aimed at teens called *Be Beautiful, Be You* and *Choosing Happiness*. She even helped produce a documentary film about her called *A Brave Heart: The Lizzie Velásquez Story*.

In her book *Dare to Be Kind*, Lizzie wrote, "You get to decide how you want to define yourself to the world." Today Lizzie continues as a motivational speaker and anti-bullying activist.

Marie Tharp

Announcement

Do you know about Marie Tharp? She created the first map of the ocean floor. Her map provided evidence supporting continental drift. Her boss dismissed the idea, calling it "girl talk." His sexist comment was wrong. Like many women, it wasn't until years later that she received recognition for her pioneering contributions in oceanography.

At (SCHOOL NAME) we remember Marie Tharp and hope your "girl talk" leads to many scientific discoveries.

Discussion Questions

- When was the last time you walked in nature?
- What does a surveyor do?
- When was the last time you looked at a map? What did that map show?
- Why do you think there were certain professions that were once more acceptable for women? Why do you think that changed during World War II?
- Why do you think Marie was bored at work?
- What do you think of Marie's boss Bruce?
- Why do you think many women scientists weren't recognized for their contributions until years later?

Marie Tharp

Marie Tharp was born on July 30, 1920. She was an only child. Her father was a soil surveyor, and because of his job, they had to move over a dozen times. When Marie was a small child, her dad would take her along, and she would play in the mud and explore nature.

In school Marie took a class called Current Science, which went over contemporary science and research projects. She attended weekend school field trips to study trees and rocks.

When Marie was fifteen, her mom died. Marie helped with the family farm the year after she graduated high school. She planned on attending college to become a teacher, like her mother. At the time, there were few professions women were allowed to go into.

When the US entered World War II, they drafted many young men. Because of this, people started to recruit women to fill in the empty positions. Marie graduated from Ohio University in 1943 with bachelor's degrees in English and music. She had taken some geology classes and was recruited by Ann Arbor's petroleum geology program. She earned a master's degree in geology and began a career in earth science. At the time, less than 4 percent of science doctorates belonged to women. Many of her first jobs left her uninspired and bored. She would take classes on the side. She earned a degree in math to help with boredom at work.

In 1952, she worked with Bruce C. Heezen mapping the ocean floor. At the time people believed the ocean floor was completely flat, and because of Marie's maps, they learned it wasn't. Marie wanted to go into the field to help measure the ocean floor, but because of a sexist myth that women were bad luck on boats, she wasn't allowed to go. So she would take the information Bruce gathered and draw maps.

A deep *V* in the middle of her maps showed the Mid-Atlantic Ridge and provided evidence to support continental drift. Her boss Bruce dismissed the idea, calling it "girl talk." His sexist comment was wrong. Bruce would publish Marie's maps and would not give her credit. Like many women, it wasn't until years later that she received recognition for her contributions in science.

In 2001 she was awarded the first annual Lamont-Doherty Heritage Award for her life's work as a pioneer of oceanography. She died of cancer when she was eighty-six.

Urvashi Vaid

Announcement

Do you know about Urvashi Vaid? She was born in India and immigrated to the US with her family as a child. At eleven she participated in the anti–Vietnam War movement, which sparked her interest in law. She became one of the top attorneys for civil rights and LGBT+ equality issues. She has written four books, one of which won the Stonewall Book Award. She believes in an inclusive movement that encompasses everyone regardless of race, class, ethnicity, age, or ability. Urvashi currently lives in Massachusetts with her partner, Kate Clinton.

Discussion Questions

- What does the acronym LGBTQIA+ mean?
- Have you ever attended a protest?
- What does it mean to be nonpartisan?
- In what ways did Urvashi put LGBTQIA+ issues in the spotlight?
- How do you think Urvashi's books helped her cause?
- What does Urvashi mean when she says, "The movement needs to be more inclusive, encompassing everyone regardless of race, class, ethnicity, age, or ability"?

Urvashi Vaid

Urvashi Vaid was born in New Delhi, India, on October 8, 1958. She immigrated to the US when she was eight years old. When she was eleven, Urvashi joined the anti–Vietnam War movement. She was always interested in politics and would read the newspaper as a child.

In 1983 she earned a degree in law from Northeastern University School of Law in Boston. That same year, she founded the Boston Lesbian/Gay Political Alliance. It was a nonpartisan group that judged candidates for political office and advocated for Boston's LGBT+ community.

In 1989 she became the Executive Director of the National Gay and Lesbian Task Force. At the time, most people weren't talking about LGBT+ issues, and Urvashi would stage events to get more media coverage on the lack of LGBT+ equality. She held many protests for reproductive rights and protests against the Persian Gulf War.

Urvashi has published four books. One of her books, *Virtual Equality*, was published in 1995 and won the Stonewall Book Award and a Lambda Liberty Award. The book expressed many ideas, including that the American gay rights movement must continue to advocate for civil equality and social change. It also pointed out how while gay white people have achieved much media attention, the same opportunities should be given to women of color and other representatives of the LGBT+ community. Her other books are *Creating Change* (2002), *It Gets Better* (2011), and *Irresistible Revolution* (2012).

She believes the LGBT+ community cannot simply win the fight for marriage equality, then slow down. The movement needs to be more inclusive, encompassing everyone regardless of race, class, ethnicity, age, and ability. She has been on the boards of many organizations, including the Ford Foundation and the Gill Foundation. Usually she is the only woman of color on the boards and stresses the need for a more diverse group to be recognized and put into positions of leadership.

Urvashi has lived with her partner, Kate Clinton, for over twenty years. Urvashi is the aunt of Alok Vaid-Menon. They are a performance artist and writer who has presented their creative work in over forty countries.

Gwendolyn Brooks

Announcement

Do you know about Gwendolyn Brooks? She was the first African American to win a Pulitzer Prize. Gwendolyn enjoyed writing poetry, and at age thirteen, her first poem, "Eventide," was published. By sixteen Gwendolyn already had seventy-five poems published. She wrote many types of poems, including ballads, sonnets, and free verse poems. She drew on musical rhythms for inspiration, and most of her poems reflected life in inner-city Chicago. In 1968 she was appointed Poet Laureate of Illinois and held the position until her death thirty-two years later.

At (SCHOOL NAME) we remember Gwendolyn Brooks and know you, too, can write Pulitzer Prize–winning poetry.

Discussion Questions

- Do you have any family lore? Explain.
- Have you written poetry? What is your favorite type of poem?
- Gwendolyn was able to focus on her writing because of winning and earning money from various organizations. What do you think of this? Should art be funded more? How do you support the arts?
- Does your state have a poet laureate? What is their name? Do you like any of their poems?

Gwendolyn Brooks

Gwendolyn Brooks was born on June 7, 1917, in Topeka, Kansas. Family lore said that her grandparents were once enslaved people who escaped and fought for the Union during the Civil War. Gwendolyn's mother was a teacher and concert pianist. She taught at the school in Topeka that later became famous for the *Brown v. Board of Education* racial desegregation case. Gwendolyn's father worked as a janitor for a music company but always hoped to become a doctor.

Gwendolyn lived in Chicago and began writing as a child. Her mother encouraged her love of poetry and writing. At age thirteen her first poem, "Eventide," was published in the magazine *American Childhood*. By sixteen Gwendolyn already had seventy-five poems published. Many poems were published in the *Chicago Defender*, an African American newspaper. Gwendolyn wrote many different types of poems, including ballads, sonnets, and free verse poems. She drew on musical rhythms for inspiration, and most of her poems reflected life in inner-city Chicago. She went to an integrated high school and saw the grave social injustice students of color faced.

She attended a two-year program at Kennedy-King College and worked as a typist for the NAACP while she pursued her writing career. She met Henry Lowington Blakely Jr. at the NAACP Youth Council branch on campus. In 1939 they married.

In 1945 she published her first book of poetry, *A Street in Bronzeville*. Bronzeville was a segregated Black neighborhood in Chicago and had one of the nation's most significant concentration of African American–owned businesses. Gwendolyn earned a Guggenheim Fellowship for her exceptional creative ability and was given money to live on while she focused on her writing.

Annie Allen was Gwendolyn's second book of poetry and was published in 1949. It focused on the life and experiences of a Black girl growing up and how her outlook on life changed with age. The book won Gwendolyn a Pulitzer Prize, making her the first African American to receive the award.

She continued her writing, publishing over ten books of poetry and one novella. In 1968 she was appointed Poet Laureate of Illinois. Poet laureates typically compose poems for special events and spread the love of poetry while also being given funds to continue their writing work. Gwendolyn held the position until her death thirty-two years later.

Ada Lovelace

Announcement

Do you know about Ada Lovelace? She was born in 1852. As a child, she excelled in mathematics. At the time, women weren't allowed to attend college, but she continued her studies under many tutors, one of which was Mary Somerville, who had the word *scientist* coined for her. Ada is often cited as the world's first computer programmer for her algebraic notes on a paper she translated. Her legacy in science and computers is still honored today. One of the first computer languages was named after her.

At (SCHOOL NAME) we remember Ada Lovelace and know you, too, can become a legendary computer programmer.

Discussion Questions

- Who takes care of you at home?
- Who are some of the teachers or mentors you've had in your life?
- How might the world be different if women had been able to attend college in Ada's time?
- How might the world of computer programming have changed if more women had been able to gain access to the information?
- Do you have two different interests that overlap? What are they?
- List some ideas of how people use math while making clothes.
- Why do you think more women aren't in computer science today?

Ada Lovelace

Ada Lovelace was born on November 27, 1852, in London, England. She was raised in a life of privileged aristocracy by her mother, Lady Byron, and grandmother, Lady Milbanke. Ada's father was the poet Lord Byron and left Ada as a baby.

Believing it would prevent Ada from catching her father's moody and unpredictable disposition, Lady Byron brought tutors to teach Ada mathematics and science, which was not the standard for women at the time. Ada was also forced to stay still for extended periods of time because her mother thought it would help Ada learn self-control.

Ada excelled in mathematics and language under various tutors, including Mary Somerville. Mary was one of the first women members of the Royal Astronomical Society, and the word *scientist* was coined for her.

At age seventeen Ada met Charles Babbage. He was a mathematician and inventor. He is known as the father of computers because of his work with a device designed to handle complex calculations. Sadly, because of sexism, Ada was not allowed to attend university but through Babbage was able to meet and study with the University of London's first math professor.

Ada is most known for her translation of the French paper *Sketches of Charles Babbage's Analytical Engine* by Luigi Menabrea, more specifically for Ada's comments that were three times longer than the piece. She added algebraic work into her notes and published the first computer program, or algorithm. Because of this, she is often cited as the world's first computer programmer.

As society required of aristocratic women, Ada kept up with fashion, but she used that interest and combined it with her mathematical analysis to develop innovative ideas in both fields. For example, she developed some insights on the Babbage machine after visiting an exhibition on the mechanical Jacquard loom. She later wrote, "We may say most aptly that the Analytical Engine weaves algebraic patterns just as the Jacquard loom weaves flowers and leaves."

Ada died at the age of thirty-six from uterine cancer. Her legacy in science and computers is still honored today. One of the first computer languages was named after her. Ironically, according to Built In at https://builtin.com/women-tech/women-in-tech-workplace-statistics, only 26 percent of computer jobs are held by women despite the field having been invented by one.

Zitkála-Šá

Announcement

Do you know about Zitkála-Šá? She was born on February 22, 1876, on the Yankton Indian Reservation in South Dakota. When Zitkála-Šá was eight, white Quaker missionaries invaded the reservation. She was taken and placed in White's Indiana Manual Labor Institute. She described the stay as deeply miserable and the school as stripping her of her heritage. At the school, she did enjoy learning to read and playing violin. She studied at a music conservatory and wrote the first indigenous opera. Today Zitkála-Šá is still remembered for her writing, music, and political activism.

Discussion Questions

- Where were the Yankton originally from? What was life like on the reservation?
- Why do you think the Quaker missionaries came? How could they have improved their school?
- When Zitkála-Šá returned, why do you think she felt that the Yankton traditions weren't completely hers anymore?
- What are some good things the General Federation of Women's Clubs did?
- Do you know any traditional Native American stories? What are some that sound interesting to read?

Zitkála-Šá

Zitkála-Šá was born February 22, 1876, on the Yankton Indian Reservation in South Dakota. Zitkála-Šá was biracial, with an indigenous Dakota mother and a French father. Zitkála-Šá's father left when she was young, leaving her to be raised by her mother and her tribe.

When Zitkála-Šá was eight, white Quaker missionaries invaded the reservation. They recruited several young children and put them in White's Indiana Manual Labor Institute. They were taught many things, like English and music, but the school was also racist. The children were not allowed to speak in their native languages and were forced to pray like the Quakers. They made Zitkála-Šá cut her traditionally long hair. She later described the whole situation as a deep misery and the school as stripping her of her heritage. Zitkála-Šá enjoyed some things at the school, like learning to read and playing violin.

When she was eleven, she returned to her mother but felt as if the Yankton traditions weren't completely hers anymore. At fifteen she wanted to learn more and returned to the institute. The school's sexist view meant those who ran it envisioned all their girl students would become housekeepers, but Zitkála-Šá wanted more. She studied piano and violin and in June 1895 earned her diploma. She gave a speech on women's rights. From there she attended Earlham College and studied at a music conservatory.

She went on to teach violin and write. Her first written works were articles criticizing the American Indian boarding school system, which forever severed many indigenous children from their cultures. She also wrote about growing up on an Indian reservation and the legends and stories of her people. Her books were among the first to bring traditional Native American stories to an English-speaking audience, and she is said to be the most influential Native American activist of the twentieth century. Later in life she published political works and created the Indian Welfare Committee of the General Federation of Women's Clubs. The group promoted civic improvements through volunteer services.

Zitkála-Šá's love of music never waned. She collaborated with composer William F. Hanson and wrote songs for *The Sun Dance Opera*, the first indigenous opera. The performance featured many members of the Ute Nation and was a big success.

Today Zitkála-Šá is still remembered for her writing, music, and political activism.

Luisa Moreno

Announcement

Do you know about Luisa Moreno? She was born in 1907 to a wealthy Guatemalan family. She attended school in California. During the Great Depression, she took up work as a seamstress. The wages were low, and her fellow Latinos faced racial segregation and discrimination. She organized, uniting the workers in a garment workers union. She used her bilingual capabilities to help workers fight for their rights and aided in the creation of over forty unions.

At (SCHOOL NAME) we remember Luisa Moreno.

Discussion Questions

- How do you think being from a wealthy family impacted Luisa?
- Do you like to read poetry? What kind of poems do you think are in *El vendedor de cocuyos* (The seller of fireflies)?
- Do you think the protest for the movie *Under a Texas Moon* would happen today? Explain.
- How are companies structured?
- What is a union?
- How are unions helpful to the workers?

Luisa Moreno

Luisa Moreno, whose original name was Blanca Rosa López Rodríguez, was born to a wealthy Guatemalan family on August 30, 1907. She attended school in Oakland, California, and later return to Guatemala as a teen. Due to sexism, women could not attend university. So Luisa formed La Sociedad Gabriela Mistral, which lobbied to allow women to seek higher education. She then moved to Mexico City and worked for a Guatemalan newspaper. At twenty she published a book of poems called El vendedor de cocuyos (The seller of fireflies).

In 1927 she moved to New York City. Shortly after, the movie Under a Texas Moon was released. It depicted racist stereotypes of Mexicans. A group of Latinos protested the movie, and the police brutalized them, killing the leader of the protest. The murder sparked more protests, which Luisa participated in. The experience motivated her to work on behalf of the Spanish-speaking community. She changed her name to Luisa Moreno to protect her family's privacy.

During the Great Depression, Luisa took up work as a seamstress. She was appalled by the horrific working conditions. The wages were low, and her fellow Latinos faced racial segregation and discrimination. She organized her fellow workers, uniting them in a garment workers union. It is hard for one worker to demand better pay from their company, but when the workers unite in a union, it forces the company to listen to the demands. Often the workers would strike, withdrawing the only power they had over the company, their labor, in order to get the company to listen. Companies do not like when their workers unionize because it cuts into the profits by fairly distributing some of the money to benefit the workers or into the hands of workers themselves. Ironically, all the profit a company earns is from the labor of the workers, thus the company should benefit the workers. To this day companies will try to illegally prevent unions from forming and demanding their fair share of profits.

In 1935 Luisa was hired by the American Federation of Labor. She used her bilingual capabilities to help workers fight for their rights. She helped unionize cigar rollers in Florida and pecan shellers in Texas. In total, she helped over forty unions take shape. Sadly, because of her powerful work assisting the common worker, she received many threatening letters. Even though she was polite and law abiding, she had to flee the US. She died on November 2, 1992.

Joseph Henry Douglass

Announcement

Do you know about Joseph Henry Douglass? He was born on July 3, 1871, and was the grandson of the well-known abolitionist Frederick Douglass. Like his grandfather and father, Joseph took up violin at a young age. When Joseph was twenty-two, he got his first big break performing at the Chicago World's Fair. For the next thirty years, he went on transcontinental tours showing his talent with the violin and inspiring others to become more interested in classical music.

At (SCHOOL NAME) we remember Joseph Henry Douglass and know you, too, can inspire others with your musical instrument.

Discussion Questions

- Have you taken interest in anything your grandparents have done?
- Why was Frederick Douglass so important? What did he do for the US?
- What is a conservatory?
- How can teachers help their students become the best they can be?

Joseph Henry Douglass

Joseph Henry Douglass was born on July 3, 1871, in Washington, DC. His grandfather was Frederick Douglass, a once enslaved man who escaped to freedom and became a well-known abolitionist. Frederick Douglass's importance and impact cannot be emphasized enough.

Like his grandfather and father, Joseph took up violin at a young age. He received training in New England at a Boston conservatory.

When Joseph was twenty-two, he got his first big break performing at the Chicago World's Fair. His grandfather helped plan the day to showcase African American talent. Joseph played, won the hearts of the people who attended, and became well known.

For the next thirty years, he went on transcontinental tours showing off his talent with the violin and inspiring other Black people to become more interested in classical music. Joseph mostly performed at Black churches and educational institutions because of the racist segregation at the time. If not for this wrong and hate-filled practice, more people would've been able to enjoy Joseph's music.

In 1914 he was the first violinist—of any race—to make recordings for the Victor Talking Machine Company. The company created gramophones that played disc recordings. While Joseph made the recordings, none were released to the general public.

Joseph also worked as an educator and conductor at Howard University in Washington, DC, and the Colored Music Settlement School in New York. He had many students, including Clarence Cameron White. Clarence was considered the foremost Black violinist of his time. Clarence is best known for his music in the play *Tambour* and the opera *Ouanga!*.

Joseph married a woman called Fannie Howard. She was a pianist and would accompany Joseph in performances. They had two children. Joseph died on December 7, 1935, at age sixty-four.

Temple Grandin

Announcement

Do you know about Temple Grandin? She was born in 1947 but was not formally diagnosed with autism until almost the nineties. Temple worked with a speech therapist and teachers who supported her needs. She earned a doctoral degree in animal science and was one of the first scientists to report that animals are sensitive to visual distractions. She continues to work for the ethical treatment of animals and is an autism spokesperson.

At (SCHOOL NAME) we remember Temple Grandin.

Discussion Questions

- How might Temple's future have looked different if she had not been born into a wealthy family?
- What are some ways you could confront the students who taunted Temple, and what steps would you take to help prevent it from happening again?
- What do you think about Temple updating her book *Thinking in Pictures*?
- While everyone can agree that the ethical treatment of animals is important, some argue against meat eating in general. What do you think about it? Why?

Temple Grandin

Temple Grandin was born on August 29, 1947, into a wealthy family. Temple's mother was able to take her to the world's leading special needs research hospital when Temple was two. Doctors first diagnosed her with brain damage and suggested speech therapy. It wasn't until Temple was in her forties that she would become formally diagnosed with autism. Because she was born into a wealthy family, she was able to get a private speech therapist and a nanny who played education games with Temple for hours. She also attended an elementary school that accommodated her needs.

Temple did not enjoy middle or high school. The students would taunt her, calling her "tape recorder" because she would repeat things she heard. On her website at https://drtemplegrandin.weebly.com/education.html, she wrote, "I could laugh about it now, but back then it really hurt." When she was fourteen, she was expelled from school for throwing a book at a student who'd taunted her. Temple then attended a private boarding school for children with behavior issues. She met William Carlock, her science teacher, who at one time worked for NASA. He encouraged her to develop her ideas and drawings.

After high school, she earned a doctoral degree in animal science. She published six books and many scientific articles. When she wrote her book *Thinking in Pictures*, she believed everyone who had autism thought like her, in visual photographic images, but later she adjusted her findings once more information was available. Her update included that some people are pattern thinkers and would make good mathematicians, chess players, musicians, and computer programmers. The last type of thinkers are verbal/logic, who think in detailed words. Their favorite subject might be history.

She worked heavily in the livestock industry and was one of the first scientists to report that animals are sensitive to visual distractions. Her development of curved corrals reduced stress and injury of animals before they are slaughtered for food. According to the University of Missouri–St. Louis website at https://www.umsl.edu/divisions/artscience/Temple%20Grandin/tempgrandin.html, she believes "we've got to give those animals a decent life, and we got to give them a painless death. We owe the animals respect."

In 2010 a film was made about her high school and early careers called *Temple Grandin*. In 2017 she was inducted into the National Women's Hall of Fame.

Temple is not married nor has any children. She thinks that emotional relationships are not a part of her. She continues to work on the ethical treatment of animals and is an autism spokesperson.

Nanyehi

Announcement

Do you know about Nanyehi? She was born in 1738 in the Cherokee town of Chota. When the American Revolution started, most Cherokees allied with the British against the colonists. Nanyehi wanted to side with the colonists, believing peace between the two peoples would be best. Nanyehi was a representative before the US treaty commissioners and wanted to end the fighting between the US and Cherokee.

At (SCHOOL NAME) we remember Nanyehi.

Discussion Questions

- What indigenous people lived where you currently live?
- Who would you have sided with in the American Revolution?
- Why do you believe the Americans wouldn't allow women in positions of power, while the Cherokee did?
- Why do you think there is a mixed and complicated view of Nanyehi today?
- How might the book published after Nanyehi's death have changed how we view her today?

Nanyehi

Nanyehi was born in 1738 in the Cherokee town of Chota. Today it is Monroe County near the border of eastern Tennessee. When she was seventeen years old, she married Tsula. They had two children.

In 1755 Nanyehi helped the Cherokee fight against the Muscogee, or Creek, people. At first, Nanyehi only helped her husband in the battle, but after he was killed, she took up her husband's rifle and led the Cherokee to victory. For her help she was awarded the title of Ghigau, or Beloved Woman. It made her the only woman voting member of the Cherokee General Council and granted her power over the fate of prisoners. She also led the Women's Council of Clan Representatives, which was one of the two governing bodies over the Cherokee Nation.

Later that same decade, Nanyehi married a white trader named Bryant Ward. She became known as Nancy Ward. They had one daughter together, and after a few years, Bryant returned to South Carolina.

When the American Revolution started, most Cherokee allied with the British against the colonists. The colonists had killed many Cherokee and taken much of their land. They wanted to expel the settlers who were encroaching on their territory. Nanyehi wanted to side with the colonists, believing peace between the two peoples would be best.

One day in the summer of 1776, Nanyehi released some white settlers and warned them of an upcoming Cherokee attack. Because of the advance notice, most women and children were saved, but the ambush killed thirteen Cherokee and injured many more.

In 1781 Nanyehi was a representative before the US treaty commissioners and wanted to end the fighting between the US and Cherokee. According to the Women and the American Story website at https://wams.nyhistory.org/settler-colonialism-and-revolution/the-american-revolution/nanyehi-nancy-ward, she said, "Let your women's sons be ours; our sons be yours. Let your women hear our words." Cherokee society valued women in decision-making, which confused the Americans. The extreme sexism at the time wouldn't allow women to participate in government.

Nanyehi's reputation is mixed. Many Americans believe her actions were honorable because of her help with the American Revolution, while to the Cherokee Nation, her reputation is more complicated. A novel written shortly after her death has also helped create the myth of Nanyehi.

Frances Perkins

Announcement

Do you know about Francis Perkins? She was the US secretary of labor from 1933 to 1945. She was the first woman and first LGBT+ person to hold a cabinet position. She established unemployment benefits, pensions, and welfare. She pushed for workers' rights and child labor laws and even created the first minimum wage. Every American has benefited from laws she shaped.

At (SCHOOL NAME) we remember Francis Perkins.

Discussion Questions

- What are some connections between chemistry and physics? What about economics and sociology?
- Why would employers lock the doors to workers' workstations? What rights do you believe workers should have?
- How has treatment for mental illness changed from Francis's time?
- How can we continue to honor and further develop the laws Francis helped establish?

Frances Perkins

Frances Perkins was born April 10, 1880. When she was young, Frances enjoyed Greek literature. In 1902 she earned a bachelor's degree in chemistry and physics, then eight years later received her master's degree in economics and sociology. During college she became interested in politics and the suffrage movement.

She witnessed the Triangle Shirtwaist Factory fire, where over 146 people died. A common practice at the time was to lock workers at their stations to prevent them from taking breaks. When the fire started, the workers were locked out of the stairwells, which would have led them to safety. Most of the people killed were Italian and Jewish women immigrants. A girl as young as fourteen died due to the poor working conditions. The tragedy encouraged Frances to lobby for better working conditions and hours as she headed the New York office of the National Consumers League.

In 1913 Frances married the economist Paul Wilson and had to defend her right to keep her maiden name in court. Six years into their marriage, Wilson started to show signs of mental illness and would be institutionalized to get help.

In 1919 Frances was confirmed as the US secretary of labor, becoming the first woman and LGBT+ person to hold a cabinet position. When she was confirmed, some senators argued against her, saying she was a radical for not taking her husband's name, which was extremely sexist. She held her position at the department for twelve years, longer than any cabinet person.

In 1922 she started a romantic relationship with Marry Harriman Rumsey. They lived together in Washington, DC, until Marry died in 1934. Due to the homophobia of the time, Frances had to mourn Marry's death privately.

During her time as the US secretary of labor, she established unemployment benefits, pensions, and welfare. She pushed for workers' rights and child labor laws and even established the first minimum wage and overtime laws. Every American, from her time in office until now, has benefited from laws she shaped.

Frances died on May 14, 1695, at age eighty-five, but every American is impacted by her legacy today.

Shirley Ann Jackson

Announcement

Do you know about Shirley Ann Jackson? She was born in 1946 and enjoyed science and math as a child. She enrolled in MIT, becoming one of fewer than twenty Black students and the only one studying theoretical physics. In 1973 she earned a doctorate in nuclear physics, becoming the first Black women to earn a doctorate from MIT and the second Black woman in the US to earn a doctorate in physics. She is currently the president of Rensselaer Polytechnic Institute. The university emphasizes science, research, and technology. Her knowledge of technology and science, along with her drive to educate others, makes the world brighter.

At (SCHOOL NAME) we remember Shirley Ann Jackson and know you can use your science and math skills to study nuclear physics.

Discussion Questions

- Are there any skills your parents or mentors help you with?
- What strategies do you think Shirley used in high school to graduate as valedictorian?
- What are some ways the white students could've made Shirley feel less isolated?
- How do you think the Black Student Union helped MIT?
- How do you like to take your notes? Do you think a sketchbook would make it easier or harder?

Shirley Ann Jackson

Shirley Ann Jackson was born on August 5, 1946, in Washington, DC. Her parents encouraged her to work hard in school, and her father helped her with science projects to expand her interest in the field. In high school Shirley excelled in math and science and graduated as valedictorian of her class in 1964.

The following fall, Shirley enrolled in MIT. She was one of fewer than twenty Black students and the only one studying theoretical physics. She described her undergrad as isolating due to the racism. White students would avoid sitting next to her in classes. She was rejected from joining study groups, even if she had already completed the homework and was happy to teach it to others. While she worked on her doctorate degree, she organized other Black students and formed the Black Student Union. They recruited more minority students to the university and helped improve their lives at MIT. She earned a doctorate in nuclear physics in 1973, becoming the first Black woman to earn a doctorate from MIT and the second Black woman in the US to earn a doctorate in physics.

After graduating, she dove into academic research, writing her notes in large sketch pads. She worked with subatomic particles and performed her experiments at labs in the US and Europe.

In 1995 President Bill Clinton appointed her to serve as the chairman of the US Nuclear Regulatory Commission. She accepted, becoming the first woman and the first Black person to hold the position. The position kept her away from her husband, fellow physicist Morris Washington, and their high-school-age son. Working with the commission, she developed a sophisticated computer to predict the risks of changes to nuclear plants.

In 1999 she became the president of the Rensselaer Polytechnic Institute, making her the first woman and first Black person to hold the position. The institute is a private research university in New York. The school emphasizes science, research, and technology. As president she fundraises for the school.

She encourages underrepresented students to attend and works closely with the Harlem Academy. Older students there spend three days a week at the university exploring science. Shirley's knowledge of technology and science, along with her drive to educate others, makes the world brighter.

Jo Ann Robinson

Announcement

Do you know about Jo Ann Robinson? She enjoyed reading as a child and graduated as valedictorian from high school. She fulfilled her dream of becoming an English teacher and taught at Alabama State College. On December 1, 1955, civil rights advocate Rosa Parks was arrested for refusing to give up her seat on a bus. Jo Ann leveraged the opportunity and created over 52,000 leaflets calling for a one-day boycott of the bus system. The boycott ended up lasting over a year and had the support of over fifty thousand people.

At (SCHOOL NAME) we remember Jo Ann Robinson.

Discussion Questions

- Jo Ann's dream career was teaching. What is your current dream career? What is one thing you have to do to achieve that?

- In 1949 Jo Ann's idea for a bus boycott was shut down. Why do you think that happened? What events might have led more people to think it was possible to desegregate busses?

- It took almost a decade after *Brown v. Board of Education* to have full desegregation in all public places. Why do you think that is?

- Rosa Parks is also said to be an inspiration for people with disabilities. Can you give examples of why this might be?

- Do you think the boycott would've gotten the results Jo Ann wanted if it had only lasted a day? What if less people had participated? Why is that?

Jo Ann Robinson

Jo Ann Robinson was born on April 19, 1912, in Georgia. She was the youngest of twelve children. The brothers and sisters worked on the family farm while attending school. Sadly, Jo Ann's father died when she was six, and the family moved to Macon, Georgia. Jo Ann enjoyed reading as a child and graduated as valedictorian from high school.

Jo Ann earned her bachelor's degree in 1934, becoming the first person in her family to graduate college. She fulfilled her dream and became an English teacher. She taught in public schools for five years while attending college to earn a master's degree in English. Eventually, Jo Ann accepted a professor position at Alabama State College in Montgomery, Alabama.

She joined the Women's Political Council, an organization that addressed racial issues in the city. They increased voter registration in Black communities and encouraged students to stay in school.

In 1949, Jo Ann sat in the front seat of an empty bus. The bus driver yelled at her, since the front was for whites only. Jo Ann feared the verbal abuse would escalate to physical and left. As a response, she thought a bus boycott to protest the racist practice of the Alabama bus segregation might be useful. She made her proposal to the Women's Political Council but was told bus segregation was a fact of life in Montgomery. The following year, Jo Ann became president of the Women's Political Council and focused their efforts on busses. She even met with the mayor and the city council, but they showed no interested in what she had to say.

In 1955 the court decision of *Brown v. Board of Education* required public schools to become desegregated. The end of segregation of all public places did not happen until almost a decade later with the Civil Rights Act of 1964.

On December 1, 1955, civil rights advocate Rosa Parks was riding on a busy bus. The white section was full enough that some whites had to stand. The bus driver ordered Rosa to move. She slid to the window seat so a standing passenger could sit next to her. The bus driver called the police, and Rosa was arrested.

Jo Ann leveraged the opportunity and created over 52,000 leaflets calling for a one-day boycott of the bus system. The boycott lasted over a year and had the support of over fifty thousand people.

Marie Maynard Daly

Announcement

Do you know about Marie Maynard Daly? She was born in 1921 to an immigrant family. Her father loved science and supported Marie's interested in the subject by giving her lots of book to read. She enrolled in a small college and lived at home to save money. She continued to work and attend school until she earned a doctorate in chemistry, becoming the first African American woman in the US to do so. It is because of her research that we understand more about the human body today.

At (SCHOOL NAME) we remember Marie Maynard Daly.

Discussion Questions

- How might the life of Marie's father have changed if he had been able to afford staying at university?
- What kind of nonfiction books do you like to read?
- The labor shortages because of the war made Marie's purpose of chemistry possible. How might the world have looked if women had always been allowed to study science fields?
- Why do you think Marie worked at Howard University?
- Many people are not able to go to college due to lack of funds, but many European countries have free college. Why do you think that is? How might it be helpful/harmful?

Marie Maynard Daly

Marie Maynard Daly was born on April 16, 1921. Her father, an immigrant from the West Indies, loved science. He attended Cornell University to become a chemist but was unable to complete his degree due to lack of funds. He encouraged Marie and showed her the wonders of science. Marie enjoyed reading, and when she visited her grandfather, she'd read the local paper detailing different scientists and their achievements. Her favorite science book was *The Microbe Hunters* by Paul de Kruif.

She enrolled in a small school called Queens College. In order to save money, she lived at home. She graduated magna cum laude with a bachelor's in chemistry in 1942. There was a labor shortage due to the war effort, and many women were given opportunities in fields usually cut off to them. Marie took advantage of the opening and studied at New York University and Columbia University. She had to tutor students for a year before she obtained funding from Columbia University to continue to work. After three years, she earned her doctorate in chemistry, becoming the first African American woman in the US to do so.

Marie taught for two years at Howard University and continued to conduct research. She studied how compounds produced in the body affect and help in digestion. Marie's research spanned four areas of chemistry: histones, protein synthesis, the relationships between cholesterol and hypertension, and creatine's uptake by muscles cells. It is because of her research that we understand the body a little better today. For example, she was the first to identify cholesterol-clogged arteries.

She was committed to increasing the enrollment of minority students in medical and graduate science programs, especially women. To honor her father, in 1988 she established a scholarship for Black students who wanted to study chemistry and physics at Queens College. Her work in the medical field was recognized by the National Technical Association. In 1999 she was considered one of the top fifty women in science, engineering, and technology by the National Technical Association.

Marie died on October 28, 2003, but her scientific achievements are still remembered today.

Raffi Freedman-Gurspan

Announcement

Do you know about Raffi Freedman-Gurspan? She was born in Honduras in 1987. Her indigenous Lenca family was unable to raise her, so she was adopted and raised by a Jewish American couple in Massachusetts. As a teenager she became interested in Norway and Scandinavia and attended Norwegian-language summer camp. In 2015 Raffi was hired by President Barack Obama, becoming the first transgender person to work as a White House staffer. Raffi continues to fight for transgender equality today.

At (SCHOOL NAME) we remember Raffi Freedman-Gurspan.

Discussion Questions

- What are some ways people can keep the Lenca language from becoming extinct?
- Are you interested in learning a new language? What language would you like to go to summer camp for?
- How do you think studying abroad shaped Raffi's career?
- What kinds of things does an LGBT liaison do to help people?
- What effects can occur because of gerrymandering?

Raffi Freedman-Gurspan

Raffi Freedman-Gurspan was born in Intibucá, Honduras, on May 3, 1987. She is part of the Lenca, the indigenous people of western Honduras and eastern El Salvador. The Lenca language is nearly extinct. Raffi's birth family was unable to raise her, so she was adopted and raised by a Jewish American couple in Massachusetts.

As a teenager Raffi became interested in Norway and Scandinavia and attended Skogfjorden, a Norwegian-language summer camp in Minnesota. In college she continued her passion for the language and spent her junior year studying at the University of Oslo in Norway in an exchange program. There she also served on the Jewish Student Union. She took international law classes with a focus on human rights and gender equality. In 2009 she earned bachelor's degrees in political science and Norwegian studies.

After graduating she joined the Massachusetts Transgender Political Coalition and worked on legislation and policy issues. In January 2010 she was hired by the mayor of Sommerville, Massachusetts, to serve as the city's LGBT liaison. She later became a legislative aide for the state representative Carl Sciortino, becoming the first openly transgender staffer for the Massachusetts House. She played a role in helping Carl pass a transgender civil rights bill in November 2011.

In 2014 Raffi was hired as a policy adviser for the National Center for Transgender Equality in Washington, DC. Her work focused on transgender people of color and those living in poverty. She covered a wide variety of topics, such as criminal justice and incarceration reform, immigration detention conditions, and developing opportunities for transgender people in the US.

The next year, Raffi was hired by President Barack Obama as an outreach and recruitment director at the White House, becoming the first transgender person to work as a staffer. Obama later appointed her to a five-year term as a member of the United States Holocaust Memorial Council.

More recently Raffi became the deputy campaign director of the All on the Line campaign, a project with a mission to end gerrymandering. Gerrymandering is the manipulation of boundaries to favor one party over the other. It is a problem solved with computer programs, but few use this method, in favor of keeping the power to manipulate elections.

Raffi continues to fight for transgender equality today.

Nella Larsen

Announcement

Do you know about Nella Larsen? She was a biracial woman born to a West Indian father and Danish immigrant mother. She spent her time working as a nurse and writing. She is recognized for her novels, *Quicksand* and *Passing*. Both are still the subjects of numerous academic studies. She is recognized as a premier novelist of the Harlem Renaissance.

At (SCHOOL NAME) we remember Nella Larsen.

Discussion Questions

- What does your family look like? Do you have any stepsiblings?
- How might Nella's move to Denmark as a child have influenced her as an adult?
- Nella had a hard time finding her place in college. Why might that have been?
- What kinds of books would you like to write? What might a book about your life be about?
- Nella suffered from depression. What are some things you can do to help a friend who might be suffering from the same illness?
- What was the Harlem Renaissance, and why is it important today?

Nella Larsen

Nella Larsen was born April 13, 1895, in Chicago. She was a light-skinned biracial woman born to a mixed-race Black father from the West Indies and an immigrant mother who was Danish. Her father died when she was two, and her mother remarried, to another white Danish immigrant. Nella had one younger half sister. They moved to a neighborhood of white immigrants, but because Nella was part Black, she faced racist discrimination and they had to relocate.

When Nella was four, her family moved to Denmark for a few years. When she was eighteen, she spent some time attending Fisk University in Tennessee. She had trouble fitting in. Most of the other students were from the South and were first-generation descendants of formerly enslaved people. Nella's immigrant/Danish childhood made it hard to connect with them. Eventually she moved back to Denmark and stayed there a few years.

In 1915 Nella graduated nursing school and moved to Alabama to work. A year later she moved to New York and earned the second-highest score on a civil service exam. She was hired as a nurse by the Bureau of Public Health. There she worked in the Bronx through the 1918 flu pandemic.

In 1919 Nella married Elmer Imes, a physicist and the second African American in the US to earn a PhD in physics. Soon after marrying, she published her first short stories. She and Elmer divorced in 1933. Nella was able to live off the alimony, but once it ran out, she had to return to nursing.

Nella worked on her first novel in 1925, having had to take a break from working due to health reasons. She became active in the Harlem literary community. In 1928 she published *Quicksand*, a novel about a biracial woman seeking acceptance and a sense of purpose. It is said to be a largely autobiographical story. Her second novel, *Passing*, is about two light-skinned women, one who marries a Black man and the other who marries a white man. Much of Nella's work was inspired by what she had to face. In 1930 she became the first Black woman awarded a Guggenheim Fellowship.

Nella struggled with depression making it hard to write and eventually had to return to nursing to support herself. She died in 1964, but even with only two published novels, her work is the subject of numerous academic studies. She is recognized as a premier novelist of the Harlem Renaissance.

Sarah Winnemucca

Announcement

Do you know about Sarah Winnemucca? She was a born in Nevada sometime around 1844. She wrote *Life among the Paiutes*, the first known autobiography written by a Native American woman. She lectured around the country, teaching others about the plight of her people caused by the constant forced migration by the US government.

At (SCHOOL NAME) we remember Sarah Winnemucca.

Discussion Questions

- How did the influence of Sarah's grandfather affect her?
- If you were the principal of the school Sarah and her sister attended, what strategies would you use to help the parents understand they shouldn't complain?
- How would you make Sarah and her sister feel more welcome at school?
- The Paiute were forced to move several times. Why do you think that is? How might Sarah's life have been different if her people hadn't been forced to move?
- How might Sarah's life have changed if the government agents had not pocketed the money owed to Sarah's people?
- Where there any other times in history where the government forced a group of people to move when they did not want to?
- How do you think Sarah's lectures and biography helped her cause?

Sarah Winnemucca

Sarah Winnemucca was born around 1844 in Nevada to an influential Paiute Native American family. It was Sarah's grandfather who set up this powerful family. After realizing the white settlers were not going to leave, he tried establishing friendly relations with his new neighbors and adopted their customs. He even fought in the Mexican-American War.

When Sarah was young, she learned English as well as Spanish and the Paiute native language. Sarah and her sister even spent a few weeks studying at a convent in San Jose, California. They would have liked to stay longer, but the racist parents of the other students complained about their children going to the same school as Native Americans. So Sarah and her sister were unfairly forced to leave, but that did not stop them from learning.

In 1859 the government established a reservation near Pyramid Lake for the Paiute people and forced them to go. Traditionally the Paiute people travel around during the year, and being forced onto the reservation meant they had to stay in one place and farm in an environment not suited for crops. The government was supposed to give the Paiute people money to help with the transition, but the agents only gave them funds for the first year and kept the remaining twenty-three years' worth for themselves.

The first winter on Pyramid Lake was harsh, and Sarah begged the nearby military leaders at Camp McDermit for help. Eventually they sent supplies, and Sarah was hired as a military interpreter. She leveraged her position and called for better treatment of her people. The men grew tired of her speaking about the wrongdoings and fired her.

In the late 1870s, the government forced the Paiute to move again, this time to Washington. It was an outrage Sarah would not stand for. She lectured about the harsh treatment of her people across California and Nevada. She, along with her father and two other tribe members, lobbied in Washington, DC, for the release of the Paiute. It was granted but did not undo the damage already done.

Sarah wrote *Life among the Paiutes*, the first known autobiography written by a Native American woman. She continued to lecture and fight for the freedoms and rights her people deserved until her death in 1891. It is because of her that we have a deeper understanding and perspective of the Paiute people.

Mary Fields

Announcement

Do you know about Mary Fields? She was a formerly enslaved person but after the Civil War, made a life for herself in the Wild West. When Mary was sixty-three, she worked for the postal service, making her the first Black woman mail carrier. Her frontier route was very dangerous, but Mary excelled. She was so beloved by the townsfolk she delivered mail to that they built a school in her honor.

At (SCHOOL NAME) we remember Mary Fields.

Discussion Questions

- Have you ever been on a steamboat? Why do you think they are not used as a major form of transportation anymore?

- What would you have done if you were in Mary's shoes, having to defend an overturned wagon from wolves?

- Mary had to leave her work with the convent because of complaints. If you were the manager, how would you have handled the situation?

- One of the heroes in a previous week was Francis Perkins, who helped establish social security and unemployment. How would Mary have benefited from these programs if they had been around while she was alive?

- What do you think about Mary's restaurants and her giving away food?

- What do you think a frontier mail carrier had to go through on a typical day?

Mary Fields

Mary Fields was born in 1832 and once grown, stood six feet tall. She was an enslaved person until slavery was outlawed in 1865. Soon after the Civil War, she worked on steamboats and even helped in steamboat races. In the 1870s she worked at the home of Judge Edmund Dunne, tending to the family's five children.

Mary was a caring person. When her friend, a nun named Mother Amadeus, was near death with pneumonia, Mary traveled to Montana to take care of her. Once Mother Amadeus recovered, Mary was hired to work at the convent. She would take care of the washing, help in the kitchen, and tend to as many as four hundred chickens.

She took her job very seriously and is said to have even yelled at people who stepped on the grass after she cut it. One day she was driving a wagon of supplies to the convent and a pack of wolves spooked her horses. The wagon overturned. The nuns would have starved without the goods. So Mary stayed by the wagon all night and kept the wolves at bay. Mary was so good at her job that she became the forewoman of the convent.

While she worked with nuns, it is said that Mary had a rough reputation of drinking in saloons and getting into gunfights with men. It's unknown why she was asked to leave the convent. Some say it was because of the complaints of men who worked under her. They did not like taking orders from her, a Black woman, and that she was paid, despite that she earned the pay from being good at her job and working for a decade at the convent.

Pushed out, Mary moved to Cascade, Montana. She opened two restaurants, but each failed. It is said the failures were due to Mary allowing people who couldn't afford to pay to eat for free.

When Mary was sixty-three, she worked for the postal service, making her the first Black woman mail carrier. She would deliver mail between Cascade and St. Peter's Mission. This frontier route was very dangerous, but Mary excelled. After retiring from postal work at seventy-one, she opened a laundry service. Her generosity continued, and she was known to give candy to the children who would pass by. Mary died in 1914 and was buried outside Cascade. She was so beloved by the townsfolk that they built a school in her honor.

Mona Hanna-Attisha

Announcement

Do you know about Mona Hanna-Attisha? Both her parents were scientists from Iraq who fled during the Saddam Hussein reign. Mona put her career on the line by becoming a whistleblower and exposing the dangerous lead levels in the Flint water supply. Nearly nine thousand children under six were exposed to the lead, which can cause learning disabilities, hearing loss, and seizures. She wrote the book *What the Eyes Don't See* about her experiences and continues to fight for public health today.

At (SCHOOL NAME) we remember Mona Hanna-Attisha.

Discussion Questions

- How might Mona's parents have influenced her decisions in life?
- What were some of the reasons the city switched to a new water supply?
- Many children suffered from lead poisoning. How might their lives be different if they hadn't been exposed?
- What could the city have done at the various stages of the pipe mishandling to correct their mistakes?

Mona Hanna-Attisha

Mona Hanna-Attisha was born in England on November 17, 1976. Both her parents were scientists from Iraq who fled during the Saddam Hussein reign. Later they immigrated to the US, and Mona grew up in Michigan.

Mona went to the University of Michigan and earned her doctorate. She studied various medical topics, such as the environment, sustainability, and public health. Her residency was at a children's hospital. She married a fellow pediatrician, and they had two daughters.

Mona is most well known for putting her career at risk by bringing to light the lead in the Flint water supply. Flint is a city in Michigan with a majority Black population. In April 2014 the city's water source was changed from Lake Huron to the Flint River. The city's lead pipes were old, and the city government failed to properly treat them to prevent the lead from going into the public water supply. The officials wanted to wait and see if these treatments were necessary.

The city covered up the toxicity of the water. On July 13, 2015, the Environmental Protection Agency sent the city a memo about the high level of lead. Brad Wurfel, spokesperson for the Michigan Department of Environmental Quality, told *Michigan Radio*, "Anyone concerned about lead in the drinking water in Flint can relax." On August 20, the city left out two of the initial reports with high levels of lead so that they could comply with the federal mandated limits.

Nearly nine thousand children under six were exposed to the lead, and thousands more adults. Lead is extremely dangerous, especially to children, and can lead to many diseases, learning disabilities, behavior issues, hearing loss, and seizures.

On September 24, 2015, Mona held a press conference detailing her findings of the lead in the water supply. The city failed to give her the necessary data to prove her findings, so she used the hospital's electronic medical records.

For months, city and state officials denied the water was a serious problem. By 2020 the governor of Michigan and eight other officials had been charged with thirty-four felony counts and seven misdemeanors. Two were also charged with involuntary manslaughter.

Mona's courage to become a whistleblower and expose the unsafe drinking water has led to better health for all the city's residents. She wrote *What the Eyes Don't See* about her experiences and continues to fight for public health today.

Felicitas Gómez Martínez de Mendez

Announcement

Do you know about Felicitas Gómez Martínez de Mendez? She was born in 1916 in the soon-to-be US territory of Puerto Rico. When Felicitas was young, her family moved to the US. When it was time for her children to attend school, they faced Juan Crow segregation laws. Felicitas wanted to give her children the best education and tried to enroll them in the whites-only school. The school allowed her lighter-skinned nephews to attend but not Felicitas's child because of her dark skin tone and Mexican last name. Felicitas's family filed a suit against the school district and won.

At (SCHOOL NAME) we remember Felicitas Gómez Martínez de Mendez.

Discussion Questions

- What does it mean to be a US territory? What are the advantages and disadvantages?
- What is Juan Crow segregation? How was it similar to Jim Crow?
- What were US internment camps?
- Why was Felicitas fighting for her kids' education?
- How did the Mendez case impact everyone in California?

Felicitas Gómez Martínez de Mendez

Felicitas Gómez Martínez de Mendez was born on February 5, 1916, in the soon-to-be US territory of Puerto Rico. When Felicitas was young, her family moved to the US, and by the time she was twelve, they'd moved to Southern California. Felicitas and her family faced racist discrimination, and even though she was from Puerto Rico, they were racialized as Mexican and faced Juan Crow segregation.

In 1936 Felicitas married Gonzalo Mendez, an immigrant from Mexico who later became a US citizen. They moved to Westminster, California, and leased a farm from the Munemitsu family. They were a Japanese American family forced to leave their home and were placed in an internment camp run by the US government. Felicitas and Gonzalo had three children, Sylvia, Gonzalo Jr., and Jerome.

There were two schools in town, the 17th Street Elementary and Hoover Elementary. The county forced school segregation. So Felicitas had to send her children to Hoover Elementary, a two-room shack, while the 17th Street Elementary provided better books and an environment created for learning. Felicitas wanted her children to have the best education. So her daughter, Sylvia, was taken by her aunt to enroll in the 17th Street Elementary along with her cousins. The school allowed Sylvia's cousins to enroll, but since Sylvia had a darker skin tone and a Hispanic last name, she was not allowed to enroll. Infuriated by the racism, her aunt took all the children out of the school and told Felicitas what had happened.

Felicitas and her husband decided to fight against the segregation. Gonzalo recruited many families, and together they voiced their displeasure. On March 2, 1945, Gonzalo along with four Mexican American fathers filed a lawsuit in federal court. The school district tried to blame a "language issue" (Bowman 2001) for the refusal to teach the students, but one of the children testified in English, demonstrating there were no issues. The court ruled in favor of the families. Then in 1947 the California governor desegrated all public schools and public places in California.

While Sylvia was able to attend the 17th Street Elementary, her white peers bullied her and called her names.

Felicitas and Gonzalo's case was used to help decide *Brown v. Board of Education*. Felicitas died on April 12, 1998.

Tammy Duckworth

Announcement

Do you know about Tammy Duckworth? She was born in Bangkok, Thailand, on March 12, 1968. Her father was American, and her mother was a Thai woman of Chinese descent. Tammy is fluent in Thai, Indonesian, and English. She joined the US Army Reserve and lost her legs in the Iraq War. Tammy did not let this stop her. On November 6, 2012, she was elected to Congress. This made her the first woman with a disability in Congress and the first US congressperson born in Thailand.

At (SCHOOL NAME) we remember Tammy Duckworth.

Discussion Questions

- What is something about Thailand you wish you knew more of?
- What are some other languages you wish you were fluent in?
- How do you think growing up in Asia helped Tammy?
- What is a Purple Heart? How do people earn the award?
- Tammy was elected to both the House of Representatives and the Senate. Why do you think she went for both?
- What is the Americans with Disabilities Act? Why is it helpful for those who need accessibility?

Tammy Duckworth

Tammy Duckworth was born in Bangkok, Thailand, on March 12, 1968. Her father was American, and her mother was a Thai woman of Chinese descent. Her father was able to date his lineage to the time of the American Revolution.

Tammy's family moved around Southeast Asia throughout her life, so she became fluent in Thai, Indonesian, and English. When she was sixteen, her family moved to Hawaii. Tammy was also a Girl Scout and won the highest award, the Girl Scout Gold Award.

She earned a bachelor's degree in political science and a master's in international affairs.

In the nineties, Tammy joined the US Army Reserve. She chose to fly helicopters because it was one of the few combat positions open to women. While studying to earn her PhD in human services, she was deployed to Iraq. The helicopter she copiloted was hit, and she lost her whole right leg and her left leg below her knee. She received a Purple Heart on December 3, 2004, and became the first American woman double amputee from the Iraq War. She retired from the military in October 2014 as a lieutenant colonel.

The Daughters of the American Revolution erected a statue in Tammy's likeness. The statue is dedicated to women veterans.

In 2006 Tammy was nominated by President Barack Obama to be the assistant secretary for public and intergovernmental affairs for the US Department of Veterans Affairs. She stayed in that position for about three years and started a program to help veterans with post-traumatic stress disorder and brain injuries.

On November 6, 2012, Tammy was elected to Congress. This made her the first woman with a disability elected to Congress and the first US congressperson born in Thailand. During her time in Congress, she is said to have saved the Americans with Disabilities Act.

Tammy was later elected senator of Illinois, and in 2018 she became the first US senator to give birth while in office. Shortly after, the Senate passed a resolution allowing a senator to bring a child under the age of one to the Senate floor during votes.

Today Tammy continues to speak out for veterans and people with disabilities.

Granville Woods

Announcement

Do you know about Granville Woods? He was born in 1856 to a part–Native American mother and African American father. When Granville was ten, he took an apprenticeship at a local machine shop. Eventually he moved to Cincinnati, Ohio, and set up business as an electrical engineer and inventor. Granville had over sixty patents and was called the "Black Edison" by the *Boston Sunday Journal*.

At (SCHOOL NAME) we remember Granville Woods.

Discussion Questions

- How much is five hundred dollars in money today?
- What could the Ohio government have done to make it easier for African Americans to be successful?
- Granville had to start working when he was ten. How good of a worker would you have been at that age?
- Is there any kind of theme you can think of with Granville's inventions?
- Why might Thomas Edison be more well known today then Granville Woods? What are some things you can do to change that?
- What are some inventions you wish were available?

Granville Woods

Granville Woods was born on April 23, 1856, in Columbus, Ohio. Granville's mother was part Native American, and his father was Black. Even though Ohio was a free state, that did not stop Black people from facing discrimination. Blacks entering the state had to pay a five-hundred-dollar bond and file evidence to prove they were free. They could not work without this permit. There were no free public schools for Black people to send their children to. Most schools available for them were run by volunteers.

Granville was able to attend school until the age of ten, but due to the racist conditions of Ohio, his family lived in poverty. So Granville needed to start work to help his family survive. He took an apprenticeship at a local machine shop.

In 1872 Granville joined the fire department and eventually became an engineer. He continued to study and worked on mills. He went to engineering college from 1876 to 1878.

In 1878 he took a job on a steamboat and within two years became chief engineer. In 1880 he moved to Cincinnati, Ohio, and set up shop as an electrical engineer and inventor. His business was called Woods Electrical Company. He created improvements on the steam boiler and invented the first electric railway. Before, the power lines ran along the train tracks, which was dangerous for pedestrians. He also invented the first telegraph system, which allowed moving trains to send out messages.

Often Granville described himself as an immigrant from Australia, thinking it would give him more respect if people thought he was from a foreign country as opposed to being African American. Still, many Black newspapers frequently expressed pride in his achievements.

Granville had over sixty patents and was sometimes called the "Black Edison," such as by the *Boston Sunday Journal*. He even sold some of his patents to the American Bell Telephone Company. Thomas Edison claimed these patents were his. Granville had to defend himself against Thomas twice in court and won both times. Eventually Thomas offered Granville a job, which he declined.

Granville died on January 30, 1910, and is still renowned for his engineering and inventions today.

Linda Sarsour

Announcement

Do you know about Linda Sarsour? Linda was the eldest of seven children and was born to Palestinian immigrant parents. Following the September 11 World Trade Center attacks, Linda become an activist, advocating for the civil rights of American Muslims. She protested the unjust police surveillance of American Muslims and advocated for the Community Safety Act in New York, which created an independent office to review police policy and widened the definition of bias-based profiling.

At (SCHOOL NAME) we remember Linda Sarsour.

Discussion Questions

- What do you think a typical day was like for Linda growing up as the oldest of seven children?

- What are some ways you could've helped Muslim Americans feel more comfortable after the September 11 attack?

- How are student holidays decided in your school district? What religions are associated with those holidays?

- How might Muslim students in New York have felt before the school holiday was established? How might they feel now with the day off?

- Why do you think Linda helps in other causes for different organizations?

Linda Sarsour

Linda Sarsour was born in Brooklyn, New York, in 1980 to Palestinian immigrant parents. Her father worked six nights a week at his corner store, Crown Heights. Linda was the eldest of seven children. She studied at John Jay High School and went to Arab-language and history classes. After graduating high school, she took classes at Kingsborough Community College to become an English teacher.

Following the September 11 World Trade Center attacks, Linda become an activist advocating for the civil rights of American Muslims. The attack fueled people's ignorance. Hate crimes and Islamophobia raged through the US. Many Muslims spoke out about how they were called slurs or were physically attacked. Others were violently murdered at the hands of bigots seeking to "avenge the US" (Religious Freedom USA).

Basemah Atweh, Linda's relative, founded the Arab American Association of New York. In 2005, Linda and Basemah attended a gala for the opening of the Arab American National Museum in Dearborn, Michigan. A tractor trailer ran their car off the road. Basemah died due to her injuries, and she had named Linda successor to the executive director position of the Arab American Association. Linda took over Basemah's vision and expanded the organization.

The Arab American Association, under Linda's lead, protested the unjust police surveillance of American Muslims. She advocated for the Community Safety Act in New York, which created an independent office to review police policy and widened the definition of bias-based profiling to include the stop and frisk practice. She also campaigned for New York public schools to have the Islamic holidays Eid al-Adha and Eid al-Fitr recognized as student holidays in 2015. Before then, the school year gave students off many Christian and Jewish holidays but no Muslim ones even though in 2008, Muslim Americans made up about ten percent of the study body.

Linda told the *New York Times*, "There are plenty of Muslim women who are backbones of the community, but they aren't usually at the forefront. There just aren't a lot of me out there—women in hijabs, doing what I do."

She helped form Muslims for Ferguson, organized Black Lives Matter protests, and was cochair of the Women's March. She continues to fight for the civil rights of Muslim Americans and others today.

Elouise Cobell

Announcement

Do you know about Elouise Cobell? She was an indigenous woman of the Blackfeet tribe. Elouise became the treasurer of the Blackfeet Nation and won a MacArthur Fellowship for her work on the Blackfeet National Bank and for promoting Native financial literacy. In 1996 she discovered many irregularities in the tribe funds held in a trust by the US government and for individual indigenous people. Elouise brought a class action suit against the Department of the Interior and won a settlement for $3.4 billion for the Blackfeet Nation.

At (SCHOOL NAME) we remember Elouise Cobell.

Discussion Questions

- Where did the Blackfeet people originally live? What was their society like before Western colonization? How much of that way of life was Elouise able to experience?

- What do you think a day in the life of Elouise growing up would have looked like?

- How is the way the government handled the Blackfeet Nation similar to how they dealt with other indigenous groups we've talked about?

- What kind of math do you think Elouise had to learn to discover the errors? Are you familiar with that type of math or still learning about it?

- Elouise won a lot of awards after her death. Why do you think that is?

Elouise Cobell

Elouise Cobell, also known as Yellow Bird Woman, was born November 5, 1945, on the Blackfeet Reservation in Montana. She grew up on her parents' cattle ranch. She had no electricity or running water, like many families on the reservation. She learned in a one-room school until she was in high school.

She attended Montana State University but had to leave before graduation due to her mother dying of cancer. After her mom's death, she moved to Seattle and married another member of the Blackfeet tribe, Alvin Cobell. They returned to the reservation to help her family.

Elouise became the treasurer of the Blackfeet Nation. She founded the Blackfeet National Bank, the first national bank located on an Indian reservation and owned by a Native American tribe. She won a MacArthur Fellowship for her work on the bank and for promoting Native financial literacy.

In 1996 she discovered many irregularities in the tribe funds held in a trust by the US government and for individual indigenous people. The government was supposed to pay fees for land leased for lumber, oil production, gas, and minerals, but Elouise found the fees weren't being received or the right amount was not coming in.

During the eighties and nineties, she attempted to seek reform for the mishandling of funds by the US government. She was unsuccessful at first, so she asked lawyer Dennis Gingold for help. Elouise, along with the Native American Rights Fund, brought a class action suit against the Department of the Interior. They won, and the decision forced reform and awarded them a $3.4 billion settlement. Elouise expressed how this amount is significantly less than the full accounting of funds owed to individual people.

Elouise died on October 16, 2011, but her fight for justice is still remembered today. In 2016 a documentary movie was made about her life called *100 Years: One Woman's Fight for Justice*, and in the same year, she was given the Presidential Medal of Freedom.

Ralph Lazo

Announcement

Do you know about Ralph Lazo? He was of Mexican American and Irish American descent. Ralph grew up in a racially diverse neighborhood and would often eat dinner at the homes of his Japanese American friends. After the Pearl Harbor attack, racist hysteria spread through the US. Anyone with Japanese heritage was forced into internment camps. These concentration camps housed over 120,000 Japanese Americans from March 1942 to November 1945. Ralph stood in solidarity with his Japanese American neighbors and joined them at the camps. He was the only unmarried non-Japanese person there. Ralph told the *Los Angeles Times* that internment was immoral, that it was wrong and he couldn't accept it.

At (SCHOOL NAME) we remember Ralph Lazo.

Discussion Questions

- What does the neighborhood where you live look like? Do a diverse group of people live there?
- If you're Filipino, what country are you from? Can you locate where that country is on a map?
- How do you think your life would have been like at the Manzanar camp? How would a typical day have been?
- Ralph was the only person who volunteered to go. Why do you think that was?
- Do you think you could sell all your possessions quickly? What do you think happened to people's homes and property if they were not able to sell?
- Some people refused to go to the internment camps. Who were they? What happened to them?

Ralph Lazo

Ralph Lazo was born on November 3, 1924. He was of Mexican American and Irish American descent. His mother died when he was young, leaving his father alone to take care of him and Ralph's younger sister. To earn money, his father had to work painting houses and murals.

Ralph grew up in a racially diverse neighborhood in Los Angeles on Temple Street. He would often eat dinner at the home of his Japanese American friends, and he played basketball on a Filipino church team.

He attended Belmont High School and was seventeen years old when the Japanese attacked Pearl Harbor on December 7, 1941. The US entered World War II, and racist hysteria ran through the nation. Anyone with Japanese heritage was forced into internment camps. These concentration camps housed over 120,000 Japanese Americans from March 1942 to November 1945.

Ralph noticed his neighbors selling their property for little money and learned how his friends were being forced against their will to move. Ralph later told the *Los Angeles Times*, "These people hadn't done anything that I hadn't done except go to Japanese language school."

Ralph stood in solidarity with his Japanese American neighbors and joined them at the camps. He was the only unmarried non-Japanese person at the camps. He later mentioned how because his skin was brown, no one in authority asked any questions and assumed his heritage. He was placed in the Manzanar camp located in the desert. The camp had eight guard towers equipped with machine guns and a fence topped with barbed wire. There was little privacy, and the toilets and showers had no partitions or stalls.

Ralph made do with the inadequate conditions. He attended the camp's high school and was even voted class president. He entertained orphaned children who had been forced to relocate there and helped deliver mail.

Since Ralph was not Japanese American, he was drafted into the military. He served as a staff sergeant in the South Pacific and helped liberate the Philippines. He received a Bronze Star Medal for his heroism in combat.

Ralph earned his master's degree in education, mentored students with disabilities, and encouraged Hispanics to attend college and vote.

Lou Sullivan

Announcement

Do you know about Lou Sullivan? He born on June 16, 1951. He enjoyed music and writing from a young age and began keeping a journal at the age of ten. When Lou was fifteen, he wrote in a journal about his identity: "I want to look like what I am but don't know what someone like me looks like. I mean, when people look at me, I want them to think—there's one of those people […] that has their own interpretation of happiness. That's what I am." His journals were later published in the book *We Laughed in Pleasure: The Selected Diaries of Lou Sullivan, 1961–1991*. Lou wore masculine fashion and in 1986 was able to fully transition into a man. Lou died of complications due to AIDS on March 2, 1991, but his activism is still being honored today.

At (SCHOOL NAME) we remember Lou Sullivan.

Discussion Questions

- Have you ever written in a journal? What kinds of things do you write / would you write in one?
- If you were moving away from your family, what items would you like them to gift you?
- Gender refers to the socially constructed characteristics associated with women, men, girls, and boys. This includes clothing, hairstyles, behaviors, and more. What are some typical things culturally connected with being a man or woman?
- How does culture influence what it means to be a man or woman?
- Are there some culturally associated things that you do that aren't typically "girl"- or "boy"-like?
- It used to be not culturally acceptable for women to wear pants. What do you think of that? How do you think it became more culturally acceptable? Can you think of other examples where what was acceptable changed?
- Lou became a mentor to many people. What are a few things you could help mentor people in?
- What other people are on the National LGBTQ Wall of Honor within Stonewall National Monument?

Lou Sullivan

Lou Sullivan was born on June 16, 1951. He grew up in Milwaukee, Wisconsin, and was the third of six children. His family was Catholic and very religious. He attended a Catholic elementary and middle school. He enjoyed music and writing from a young age and began keeping a journal at the age of ten.

When Lou was fifteen, he wrote in a journal about his identity: "I want to look like what I am but don't know what someone like me looks like. I mean, when people look at me, I want them to think—there's one of those people [...] that has their own interpretation of happiness. That's what I am." His journals were later published in the book *We Laughed in Pleasure: The Selected Diaries of Lou Sullivan, 1961–1991*.

He was interested in gender roles and would often play male roles in games. Even his short stories explored gender from a man's perspective.

In 1973 Lou began to identify as male, making him a female-to-male (FTM) transgender person. Soon after, he realized he had to move from Milwaukee to have access to the healthcare he needed. He moved to San Francisco. His family supported the move, gifting him a suit and his grandfather's pocket watch.

Lou wore masculine fashion and described himself as a gay man. At the time, it was expected that transgender people should adopt a stereotypical relationship with someone of the opposite gender. Since Lou identified as gay, he was repeatedly denied his gender confirmation surgery.

After the death of his brother, Lou found doctors and therapists who accepted his sexuality and in 1986 was able to fully transition into a man.

Lou wrote the first guidebook for FTM people and a biography about fellow FTM person Jack Bee Garland. Lou was active in the Gateway Gender Alliance, one of the first social/educational organizations for transgender people. He was also a founding member and board member of the GLBT Historical Society in San Francisco. Lou lobbied for the American Psychiatric Association to recognize the existence of gay trans men. He was determined to remove sexual orientation from the criteria to have transition surgery.

Lou died of complications due to AIDS on March 2, 1991, but his activism is still being honored today. In 2019 he was inducted onto the National LGBTQ Wall of Honor within Stonewall National Monument.

Farida Bedwei

Announcement

Do you know about Farida Bedwei? She was born in Lagos, Nigeria, in 1979. Growing up Farid lived in Dominica, Grenada, and the UK before her family settled in Ghana. She was diagnosed with cerebral palsy at a young age. Cerebral palsy is a group of disorders affecting a person's ability to stay balanced and move. Farida enjoyed computers, and at fifteen she enrolled in a one-year computer class. She was the youngest in her class, and it enabled her to skip high school. Now Frida is a computer engineer and businesswoman.

At (SCHOOL NAME) we remember Farida Bedwei.

Discussion Questions

- In what ways does the United Nations Development Programme help people?
- Has cerebral palsy affected your life? If not, how might your life look different if you had it?
- What is ableism? What would you say if you saw someone being ableist?
- What features does your school have to accommodate people with mobility issues?
- How often do you use a computer? Why would knowing more about how computers work help you in your everyday life?
- If you wrote a superhero comic, what would your character be like? What would be their superpower?

Farida Bedwei

Farida Bedwei was born in Lagos, Nigeria, on April 6, 1979. Her father worked with the United Nations Development Programme. The program works in over 177 nations and promotes connecting countries to knowledge and resources to help people build better lives for themselves. Growing up Farida lived in Dominica, Grenada, and the UK. Her family settled in Ghana when she was nine years old.

She was diagnosed with cerebral palsy at a young age. Cerebral palsy is a group of disorders affecting a person's ability to stay balanced and move. It is the most common motor disability of childhood. One in about every 345 children is diagnosed with cerebral palsy. Farida told the World Cerebral Palsy Day website at https://worldcpday.org/meet-farida-bedwei-superhero-and-software-engineer, "Growing up, I knew I had limitations, but I was taught to try and surmount them."

At twelve she was sent to the first government school in Ghana. When she entered high school, she realized the school had bad terrain, which made it hard for her to use her crutches to move around. This ableism prevented her from continuing into the government high school. Farida enjoyed computers, and at fifteen she enrolled in a one-year computer class at St. Michael's information technology center. She was the youngest in her class, and it enabled her to skip high school.

She continued her education in computers and public management, getting certifications in the UK and one-year degrees from a school in Ghana. She began her career as a software developer and by 2010 was a senior software architect. She has described her education as unconventional because she lived in a country without inclusive schools but says she made it work.

In 2011 she set up her own company and led the creation of gKudi, web-based micro banking software. It was extremely successful.

In 2015 she published a biography called *Definition of a Miracle*. She also created a superhero called Karmzah, who also has cerebral palsy. Karmzah's walking crutches are her superpower, and she fights people who want to destroy her local community and African society.

When asked by the World Cerebral Palsy Day website at https://worldcpday.org/meet-farida-bedwei-superhero-and-software-engineer about what she would tell children with disabilities, she said, "Accept and love yourself for who you are. Don't waste your time wishing you didn't have this condition. Rather, find ways to attain greater heights with your disabilities."

Amanda Nguyen

Announcement

Do you know about Amanda Nguyen? She was born in 1991 in California. She earned a bachelor of arts from Harvard University in 2013. She formed the nonprofit Rise, which aims to protect the civil rights of sexual assault survivors. According to the Igitenational.org website, she named her organization Rise to "remind us that a small group of thoughtful, committed citizens can rise up and change the world." So far Rise has helped pass thirty-three laws.

At (SCHOOL NAME) we remember Amanda Nguyen.

Discussion Questions

- How did you feel when you learned what happened to Amanda?
- Where, if at all, does sexism come up in your everyday life?
- What does "undue burden" mean? List some examples that have happened to you or that you know about.
- What is a statute of limitations? Do you think it is a good or bad thing to have? Why?
- Name examples of small groups of thoughtful, committed citizens that change the world?
- What is a hate crime?

Amanda Nguyen

Amanda Nguyen was born in 1991 in California. She earned a bachelor of arts from Harvard University.

In 2013 she was raped while at college. A sexual assault case could last years and take up much of the victim's time and resources, not to mention the traumatic event would have to be relived at trial. In Massachusetts there was a fifteen-year statute of limitations for rape, but if charges were not pressed within six months, the evidence of the rape kit would be destroyed. This system placed an undue burden on survivors, forcing them to press charges when some of them might not be ready.

Amanda wanted to help other sexual assault survivors and formed the nonprofit Rise. According to the website ignitenational.org at https://ignitenational.org/blog/amanda-nguyen-is-an-ignite-leader-on-fire, she named the organization Rise to "remind us that a small group of thoughtful, committed citizens can rise up and change the world."

Rise gave Amanda a platform and the ability to catch the attention of people in government. In 2015 she met with Jeanee Shaheen, a senator from New Hampshire. Amanda talked with her about the unfair laws that did not protect the civil rights of sexual assault survivors at the federal level. Amanda wanted the evidence of every rape kit preserved for the duration of the statute of limitations. In 2016 the bill ensuring this was signed into law.

In 2017 she was a Women's March honored guest and speaker, and she has been featured in numerous publications, including *Forbes* as part of the "30 under 30" and the *Guardian* in "The Frederick Douglass 200."

In 2018 Amanda was nominated for the Nobel Peace Prize. She wants to expand survivorship laws throughout all fifty states and has traveled to Japan to promote similar laws. So far Rise has helped pass thirty-three laws.

On February 2, 2021, she spoke out against a spike in anti-Asian hate crimes happening throughout the United States sparked by the COVID-19 pandemic. She was upset about the lack of media coverage of these hate crimes. She wanted to make a call to action for the media to uplift Asian stories.

Rise and Amanda continue to fight for civil rights today.

About the Author

International best-selling author Stephanie Bazzell has been in education for over a decade. She has worked in sleepy towns and bustling cities. She believes consistent small changes add up to big results! Her work with various schools and organizations has brought about positive radical change, improving cultural proficiency, equality, diversity, and inclusion in schools and businesses. Stephanie is an atheist, queer woman and is a sought-after speaker. She currently lives in Dallas, Texas, with her husband and calico cat. If you would like to book Stephanie for your convocation or a consult with your organization, contact her at www.stephaniebazzell.com.

Stephanie is available in person or online to work with your group on cultural proficiency, equality, diversity, and inclusion. Book her today for…

- Consulting
- Training
- Speaking

Speaking topics include the following:
- creating a more culturally proficient, inclusive, and diverse campus
- science-based wellness for teachers

Bibliography

Charles Henry Turner

Abramson, Charles. "Charles Henry Turner: A Brief Biography." Accessed April 9, 2021. https://psychology.okstate.edu/museum/turner/turnerbio.html.

African American History Program. "Charles Henry Turner." National Academy of Sciences. Accessed April 9, 2021. http://www.cpnas.org/aahp/biographies/charles-henry-turner.html.

Giurfa, Martin, and Maria Gabriela de Britos Sanchez. "Black Lives Matter: Revisiting Charles Henry Turner's Experiments on Honey Bee Color Vision." *Current Biology* 30, no. 20 (October 19, 2020): R1235–R1239. https://doi.org/10.1016/j.cub.2020.08.075.

Bessie Coleman

Public Broadcasting Service. "Bessie Coleman." WGBH Educational Foundation. Accessed April 9, 2021. https://www.pbs.org/wgbh/americanexperience/features/flygirls-bessie-coleman.

Rudd, Thelma. "Yesterday, Today and Tomorrow." The Official Website of Bessie Coleman. Accessed April 9, 2021. http://www.bessiecoleman.org/bio-bessie-coleman.php.

Jovita Idár

Agresta, Michael. "Forgotten for Over a Century, Border Hero Jovita Idár Is Rediscovered by Her Hometown of Laredo." *Texas Observer*, February 1, 2021. https://www.texasobserver.org/forgotten-for-over-a-century-border-hero-jovita-idar-is-rediscovered-by-her-hometown-of-laredo.

Alexander, Kerri Lee. "Jovita Idár." National Women's History Museum. 2019. https://www.womenshistory.org/education-resources/biographies/jovita-idar.

Vera Rubin

National Science Foundation. "Vera Rubin (19282016)." Accessed April 9, 2021. https://www.nsf.gov/news/special_reports/medalofscience50/rubin.jsp.

Soter, Steven, and Neil deGrasse Tyson, eds. "Vera Rubin and Dark Matter." In *Cosmic Horizons: Astronomy at the Cutting Edge*. New Press, 2000. American Museum of Natural History. https://www.amnh.org/learn-teach/curriculum-collections/cosmic-horizons-book/vera-rubin-dark-matter.

Mae Jemison

Biography. "Mae C. Jemison." A&E Television Networks. April 27, 2017. https://www.biography.com/astronaut/mae-c-jemison.

Patsy Takemoto Mink

Alexander, Kerri Lee. "Patsy Mink." National Women's History Museum. 2019. https://www.womenshistory.org/education-resources/biographies/patsy-mink.

US House of Representatives. "MINK, Patsy Takemoto." History, Art & Archives. Accessed April 9, 2021. https://history.house.gov/People/detail/18329.

Peter Salem

Freedom's Way National Heritage Area. "Peter Salem: Patriot of Color." Exploring Patriots' Day Stories. Accessed April 9, 2020. http://freedomsway.org/peter-salem-patriot-of-color%E2%80%A8/.

Hannigan, John. "Patriots of Color." National Park Service. US Department of the Interior. Accessed April 9, 2021. https://www.nps.gov/mima/patriotsofcolor.htm.

Octavia Spencer

Guglielmi, Jodi. "Octavia Spencer on Growing Up with Dyslexia." *People*, March 29, 2017. https://people.com/celebrity/octavia-spencer-on-growing-up-with-dyslexia.

Wright, Lexi Walters. "Celebrity Spotlight: Dyslexia Can't Stop Octavia Spencer's Success." *Understood*, October 22, 2020. https://www.understood.org/en/learning-thinking-differences/personal-stories/famous-people/celebrity-spotlight-dyslexia-cant-stop-octavia-spencers-success.

Annie Malone Turnbo

Blanco, Lydia. "The Grandniece of Millionaire and Beauty Pioneer Annie Turnbo Malone Is Sharing Her Story." *Black Enterprise*, May 4, 2020. https://www.blackenterprise.com/the-grandniece-of-millionaire-and-beauty-pioneer-annie-turnbo-malone-is-sharing-her-story.

Nittle, Nadra. "Meet Annie Turnbo Malone, the Hair Care Entrepreneur Trump Shouted Out in His Black History Month Proclamation." *Vox*, February 15, 2019. https://www.vox.com/the-goods/2019/2/15/18226396/annie-turnbo-malone-hair-entrepreneur-trump-black-history.

Lizzie Velásquez

Velásquez, Lizzie. *Dare to Be Kind: How Extraordinary Compassion Can Transform Our World*. New York: Hachette Books, 2018.

Velásquez, Lizzie. "How Do You Define Yourself?" Filmed December 2013 at TEDxAustinWomen, Austin, Texas. Video, 13:10. https://www.ted.com/talks/lizzie_velasquez_how_do_you_define_yourself?language=en.

Marie Tharp

Tharp, Marie. "Connect the Dots: Mapping the Seafloor and Discovering the Mid-ocean Ridge." In *Lamont-Doherty Earth Observatory of Columbia: Twelve Perspectives on the First Fifty Years 1949–1999*. Lamont-Doherty Earth Observatory: 1999. Woods Hole Oceanographic Institution. April 1, 1999. https://www.whoi.edu/news-insights/content/marie-tharp.

The Mariners' Museum and Park. "Marie Tharp." The Ages of Exploration. Accessed April 9, 2021. https://exploration.marinersmuseum.org/subject/marie-tharp.

Urvashi Vaid

GLSEN. "Women's History Month Heroes: Urvashi Vaid." Accessed April 9, 2021. https://www.glsen.org/blog/womens-history-month-heroes-urvashi-vaid.

Urvashi Vaid. "About." Accessed April 9, 2021. https://urvashivaid.net/wp/?page_id=2.

The Vaid Group. "Team." Accessed April 9, 2021. https://thevaidgroup.com/team.

Gwendolyn Brooks

Poetry Foundation. "Gwendolyn Brooks." Accessed April 9, 2021. https://www.poetryfoundation.org/poets/gwendolyn-brooks.

Ada Lovelace

Daley, Sam. "Women in Tech Statistics Show the Industry Has a Long Way to Go." Built In. Accessed April 9, 2021. https://builtin.com/women-tech/women-in-tech-workplace-statistics.

MIT Press. "Celebrating Ada Lovelace." The MIT Press. October 11, 2016. https://mitpress.mit.edu/blog/celebrating-ada-lovelace.

Reynolds, Lauren Mackenzie. "Meet Ada Lovelace, the World's First Computer Programmer." Massive Science. August 10, 2018. https://massivesci.com/articles/ada-lovelace-first-programmer-science-heroes.

Zitkála-Šá

National Park Service. "Zitkala-Ša (Red Bird / Gertrude Simmons Bonnin)." US Department of the Interior. Accessed April 9, 2021. https://www.nps.gov/people/zitkala-sa.htm.

Women and the American Story. "Life Story: Zitkala-Sa, aka Gertrude Simmons Bonnin (1876–1938)." New-York Historical Society. Accessed February 11, 2021. https://wams.nyhistory.org/modernizing-america/xenophobia-and-racism/zitkala-sa.

Luisa Moreno

Brooklyn Museum. "Luisa Moreno." Elizabeth A. Sackler Center for Feminist Art. Accessed April 9, 2021. https://www.brooklynmuseum.org/eascfa/dinner_party/heritage_floor/luisa_moreno.

National Museum of American History. "The Case of Luisa Moreno." Accessed January 15, 2021. https://americanhistory.si.edu/american-enterprise/new-perspectives/luisa-moreno.

Joseph Henry Douglass

African American Registry. "Violinist Joseph Douglass Born." July 3, 1869. https://aaregistry.org/story/violinist-joseph-douglass-born.

Temple Grandin

Grandin, Temple. "The World Needs All Kinds of Minds." Filmed February 2010 at TED2010, Long Beach, California. Video, 19:27. https://www.ted.com/talks/temple_grandin_the_world_needs_all_kinds_of_minds?language=en.

Temple Grandin, PhD. "Dr. Temple Grandin of CSU Named One of the Top 10 College Professors in the Country." Accessed April 9, 2021. https://www.templegrandin.com.

University of Missouri—St. Louis. "Temple Grandin." College of Arts and Sciences. Accessed April 9, 2021. https://umsl.edu/divisions/artscience/Temple%20Grandin/tempgrandin.html.

Nanyehi

Klibanoff, Caroline, and Allyson Schettino. "Nanyehi 'Nancy' Ward Helped Lead the Cherokee Nation as a Teenager." *Teen Vogue*, November 30, 2020. https://www.teenvogue.com/story/who-was-nanyehi-nancy-ward.

Women and the American Story. "Life Story: Nanyehi Nancy Ward (1738–1822)." New-York Historical Society. Accessed February 11, 2021. https://wams.nyhistory.org/settler-colonialism-and-revolution/the-american-revolution/nanyehi-nancy-ward.

Frances Perkins

Downey, Kirstin. *The Woman behind the New Deal: The Life and Legacy of Frances Perkins, FDR's Secretary of Labor and His Moral Conscience*. New York: Anchor Books, 2009.

Frances Perkins Center. Accessed April 9, 2021. https://francesperkinscenter.org.

Shirley Ann Jackson

Rensselaer Polytechnic Institute. "Biography: Shirley Ann Jackson, PhD." Accessed April 9, 2021. https://president.rpi.edu/president-biography.

Schaffer, Amanda. "The Remarkable Career of Shirley Ann Jackson." *MIT Technology Review*, July 28, 2020. https://www.technologyreview.com/2017/12/19/146775/the-remarkable-career-of-shirley-ann-jackson.

Jo Ann Robinson

National Museum of African American History and Culture. "Jo Ann Robinson: A Heroine of the Montgomery Bus Boycott." Our American Story. Smithsonian. Accessed August 2, 2019. https://nmaahc.si.edu/blog-post/jo-ann-robinson-heroine-montgomery-bus-boycott.

Marie Maynard Daly

Science History Institute. "Marie Maynard Daly." Accessed June 15, 2020. https://www.sciencehistory.org/historical-profile/marie-maynard-daly.

Raffi Freedman-Gurspan

Mormann, Nicole. "White House Hires First Openly Transgender Staffer." *TakePart*, August 18, 2015. http://www.takepart.com/article/2015/08/18/transgender-official.

Puno, and Raffi Freedman-Gurspan. "Raffi Freedman-Gurspan on How to Advocate for a Seat at the Table." Girlboss Radio. March 16, 2021. Podcast, 56:00. https://www.girlboss.com/read/raffi-freedman-gurspan.

Swint, Kat. "Raffi Freedman-Gurspan." Wonder Women. Accessed April 9, 2021. https://www.wndrwmn.com/raffi-freedmangurspan.

The White House. "White House Author: Raffi Freedman-Gurspan." US National Archives and Records Administration. Accessed April 9, 2021. https://obamawhitehouse.archives.gov/blog/author/raffi-freedman-gurspan.

Nella Larsen

Johnson, Doris Richardson. "Nella Larsen (1891–1963)." BlackPast. January 19, 2007. https://www.blackpast.org/african-american-history/larsen-nella-1891-1963.

Wertheim, Bonnie. "Nella Larsen." Overlooked. *New York Times*. Accessed March 8, 2018. https://www.nytimes.com/interactive/2018/obituaries/overlooked-nella-larsen.html.

Mary Fields

Amspacher, Shelby. "Stagecoach Mary Fields." National Postal Museum. Smithsonian. April 1, 2020. https://postalmuseum.si.edu/stagecoach-mary-fields.

Mona Hanna-Attisha

Booker, Brakkton. "Former Michigan Gov. Rick Snyder Charged in Flint Water Crisis." *NPR*, January 13, 2021. https://www.npr.org/2021/01/13/956592508/new-charges-in-flint-water-crisis-including-former-michigan-gov-rick-snyder.

Malewitz, Jim, and Craig Mauger. "He Told Flint to 'Relax.' Now, Michigan Is Paying Him to Lead Media Training." *Bridge Michigan*, July 11, 2018. https://www.bridgemi.com/michigan-environment-watch/he-told-flint-relax-now-michigan-paying-him-lead-media-training.

Mona Hanna-Attisha. "Dr. Mona Hanna-Attisha MD, MPH, FAAP." Accessed April 9, 2021. https://monahannaattisha.com/about.

Smith, Lindsey. "Leaked Internal Memo Shows Federal Regulator's Concerns about Lead in Flint's Water." *Michigan Radio*, July 13, 2015. https://www.michiganradio.org/post/leaked-internal-memo-shows-federal-regulator-s-concerns-about-lead-flint-s-water.

Felicitas Gómez Martínez de Mendez

Bowman, Kristi L. "The New Face of School Desegregation." *Duke Law Journal* 50, no. 6 (2001): 1751–1808. https://scholarship.law.duke.edu/dlj/vol50/iss6/5.

Laboy, Suset. "Meet Felicitas 'La Prieta' Mendez: Pioneer in the Struggles for Desegregation." Center for Puerto Rican Studies. Hunter College. *Centro Voices*, February 4, 2015. https://centropr.hunter.cuny.edu/centrovoices/chronicles/meet-felicitas-la-prieta-mendez-pioneer-struggles-desegregation.

Madrid, E. Michael. "The Unheralded History of the Lemon Grove Desegregation Case." *Multicultural Education* 15, no. 3 (Spring 2008): 15–19. https://files.eric.ed.gov/fulltext/EJ793848.pdf.

Tammy Duckworth

Dorsainvil, Monique. "Meet the Women of the Administration: Tammy Duckworth." The White House. March 4, 2011. https://obamawhitehouse.archives.gov/blog/2011/03/04/meet-women-administration-tammy-duckworth.

Johnson, Rebecca. "Senator Tammy Duckworth on the Attack That Took Her Legs—and Having a Baby at 50." *Vogue*, September 12, 2018. https://www.vogue.com/article/tammy-duckworth-interview-vogue-october-2018-issue.

Tammy Duckworth for US Senate. "Meet Tammy Duckworth." Accessed March 26, 2021. https://tammyduckworth.com/meet-tammy.

US Senator Tammy Duckworth for Illinois. "About Tammy." Accessed April 9, 2021. https://www.duckworth.senate.gov/about-tammy/biography.

Granville Woods

Biography. "Granville T. Woods." A&E Television Networks. January 19, 2018. https://www.biography.com/inventor/granville-t-woods.

Boston Sunday Journal. "'Black Edison's' Patents." April 20, 1902.

Ohio History Connection. "Granville T. Woods." Ohio History Central. Accessed April 9, 2021. https://ohiohistorycentral.org/w/Granville_T._Woods.

Linda Sarsour

"Bio—Linda Sarsour." Linda Sarsour. Accessed April 9, 2021. https://www.lindasarsour.com/about.

Feuer, Alan. "Linda Sarsour Is a Brooklyn Homegirl in a Hijab." *New York Times*, August 7, 2015. https://www.nytimes.com/2015/08/09/nyregion/linda-sarsour-is-a-brooklyn-homegirl-in-a-hijab.html.

InfluenceWatch. "Linda Sarsour." Accessed April 9, 2021. https://www.influencewatch.org/person/linda-sarsour/.

Iowa State University. "Linda Sarsour." Archives of Women's Political Communication. Accessed April 9, 2021. https://awpc.cattcenter.iastate.edu/directory/linda-sarsour.

Religious Freedom USA. "What Is Islamophobia? Understanding the Anti-Muslim Sentiment through the Lens of Westerners." October 27, 2020. https://religiousfreedomusa.org/what-is-islamophobia.

Women's Media Center. "Linda Sarsour ." WMC SheSource. Accessed April 9, 2021. https://www.womensmediacenter.com/shesource/expert/linda-sarsour.

Elouise Cobell

Melinda, Janko. "Elouise Cobell: A Small Measure of Justice." *American Indian* 14, no. 2 (Summer 2013). https://www.americanindianmagazine.org/story/elouise-cobell-small-measure-justice.

Rothberg, Emma. "Elouise Cobell ('Yellow Bird Woman')." National Women's History Museum. Accessed April 9, 2021. https://www.womenshistory.org/education-resources/biographies/elouise-cobell-yellow-bird-woman.

Ralph Lazo

History. "Japanese Internment Camps." A&E Television Networks. October 29, 2009. https://www.history.com/topics/world-war-ii/japanese-american-relocation.

Los Angeles Almanac. "Ralph Lazo: Friendship in the Face of Injustice." Given Place Media. Accessed April 9, 2021. http://www.laalmanac.com/history/hi07se.php.

University of California, Los Angeles. "Ralph Lazo '40s." UCLA: Our Stories, Our Impact. Institute for Research on Labor and Employment. Accessed April 9, 2021. https://ourstoriesourimpact.irle.ucla.edu/ralph-lazo.

Lou Sullivan

Gender Spectrum. "Understanding Gender." Accessed April 16, 2020. https://genderspectrum.org/articles/understanding-gender.

GLBT Historical Society. "Primary Source Set: Lou Sullivan." Accessed April 9, 2021. https://www.glbthistory.org/primary-source-set-lou-sullivan.

National LGBTQ Task Force. "National LGBTQ Wall of Honor Unveiled at Historic Stonewall Inn." June 27, 2019. https://www.thetaskforce.org/nationallgbtqwallofhonortobeunveiled.

Sullivan, Lou. *We Both Laughed in Pleasure: The Selected Diaries of Lou Sullivan 1961–1991*. Edited by Ellis Martin and Zach Ozma. New York: Nightboat Books, 2019.

Farida Bedwei

Centers for Disease Control and Prevention. "What Is Cerebral Palsy?" National Center on Birth Defects and Developmental Disabilities. Last reviewed December 31, 2020. https://www.cdc.gov/ncbddd/cp/facts.html.

Eisenmenger, Ashley. "Ableism 101: What It Is, What It Looks Like, and What We Can Do to Fix It." Access Living, December 12, 2019. https://www.accessliving.org/newsroom/blog/ableism-101.

Her Abilities Award. "Farida Bedwei: Juror Profile." Accessed April 9, 2021. https://www.her-abilities-award.org/farida-bedwei.

Jonathan. "Meet Farida Bedwei: Superhero and Software Engineer." World Cerebral Palsy Day. October 8, 2020. https://worldcpday.org/meet-farida-bedwei-superhero-and-software-engineer.

Amanda Nguyen

Dill, Kathryn, Chris Denhart, Dan Fisher, and Avik Roy, eds. "Forbes 30 under 30: Law and Policy." *Forbes*, 2017. https://www.forbes.com/30-under-30-2017/law-policy.

Liu, Jennifer. "How Millennial Nobel Prize Nominee Amanda Nguyen's Viral Video Sparked Coverage of Anti-Asian Racism." *CNBC*, March 1, 2021. https://www.cnbc.com/2021/03/01/amanda-nguyens-viral-video-raises-awareness-of-anti-asian-racism.html.

Nguyen, Amanda (amandangocnguyen). "Last Thursday an 84 year old Thai American was MURDERED in San Francisco. He died this week. On Wednesday a 64 year old Vietnamese grandmother was assaulted in…" Instagram video, February 5, 2021. https://www.instagram.com/p/CK7vwR2HNM7.

Rise. Accessed April 9, 2021. https://www.risenow.us.

Rogers, Kirsten. "Amanda Nguyen Is an IGNITE Leader on Fire," March 31, 2021. https://ignitenational.org/blog/amanda-nguyen-is-an-ignite-leader-on-fire.

www.ingramcontent.com/pod-product-compliance
Lightning Source LLC
Chambersburg PA
CBHW081754100526
44592CB00015B/2429